AN INTRODUCTION TO CONTEMPORARY AESTHETICS

CONTEMPORARY AESTHETICS

A Philosophical Analysis

R.A. Sharpe

ST. MARTIN'S PRESS   New York

Library of Congress Card Catalog Number 82-42931
ISBN 0-312-16633-8

Contents

Preface   vii

1   Is 'Art' a Partisan Concept?   1

2   Classifying the Arts   6

3   What Art Is!   27

    Neo-Wittgensteinism theories   28
    Art world theories   30
    Aesthetic attention   36
    Representation   49
      Illusion, pretence and dramatic representation   50
      Pictorial representation   56
      A good likeness   64
      Literature and representation   75

4   Expressionism   93

5   Metaphors of Interpretation and Interpretation of Metaphors   116

    Interpreting   119
    Intentions   121
    The variety of interpretations   132
    The topography of interpretations   138
    Critical reasons and the hermeneutic circle   141
    The interpretation of metaphor   149
    Conclusion   159

6   Comparative Judgement   161

Epilogue   183
Notes   187
Index   195

Preface

Philosophers are, I sometimes think, constitutionally in-
capable of writing textbooks since, through training and
inclination, they are unable to avoid their own opinions
from obtruding at every corner in the argument. This
book is no exception. I depart from many other writers in
my treatment of interpretation and dramatic representation, for instance. More particularly there is an ines-
capable flavour of the exotic which derives from my
interest in both hermeneutics and structuralism.

However, these idiosyncrasies apart, I have tried to
present a picture of how the main problems in aesthetics
appear in the last quarter of a century particularly rich in
philosophical achievement, an account which will be
intelligible and, I hope, interesting both to students of
philosophy and to the many students of other disciplines
who take aesthetics as an optional subject. As in the
philosophy of religion, the teacher of aesthetics begins
with the great advantage that his audience will have
thought in at least a rudimentary way upon the principal
themes of the subject, on the diversity of taste and the
apparent impenetrability of a concept of 'art' which embraces both the Mona Lisa and piles of bricks. Equally, I
know of no one totally devoid of some aesthetic interest,
be it gardening, stamp collecting or rock music (though
Immanuel Kant has been suggested as an exception).

In my view nothing equals the value and importance of
the arts. It does not follow from this that aesthetics is the
most important branch of philosophy because it could be
the case that the problems of aesthetics are jejune and
easily dealt with. However, I do think that the problems of
aesthetics are interesting and bear closely on our

practical concerns in the arts, and the position I give the arts in human society means that other branches of philosophy must serve a subsidiary role. The study of ethics and politics, for example, is important mainly because it examines issues that arise from our need to construct a society sufficiently stable for the arts to be cultivated in decency and leisure.

One other general point which properly belongs to the preface. My concern is for the distinctions that critics and artists make when they are not being self-consciously 'philosophical'. I think, and here I have been influenced by Austin, that where there is an unreflective distinction made by a consensus it is likely to have a rationale. If musicians talk about one conductor repeating another's interpretation, then, by implication, this tells us a great deal about the ontology of the performing arts. Conceptual legislation is of little interest to me.

ACKNOWLEDGEMENTS

A part of Chapter 1 appeared as 'Type, Token, Interpretation and Performance' in *Mind*, July 1979; parts of Chapter Five as 'Interpreting Art' in the Proceedings of the Aristotelian Society, *Supplementary Volume LV* 1981; and parts of Chapter Six as 'A Transformation of a Structuralist Theme', in the *British Journal of Aesthetics*, 1978. I am indebted to the editors of these journals for permission to publish.

I thank Mrs Gwen Evans for typing this book and its several ancestors. My intellectual debts both to other philosophers and to my students are too many to cite. However I must record my gratitude to David Cockburn for reading a late version with great care.

1

Is 'Art' a Partisan Concept?

What makes an artefact a work of art? During the course of this book we shall examine theories about what makes a painting, a novel or a symphony different from the other creations of mankind, theories which vary from the venerable idea that art is an imitation or a representation of people, their actions and the natural setting of mankind, to the more modern view that art is expressive of the mind or personality of its creator. These theories share at least one common feature, the assumption that art has a nature which can be discovered. It has an essence. As we shall see, not every modern writer on aesthetics shares this assumption. Followers of Wittgenstein, for example, have argued that it is a fundamental error to suppose that art possesses such an essence. Their scepticism is shared by a group of thinkers who are, in other respects, very distant from the methods and presuppositions of Wittgensteinism and whose interest in art is overtly political. These critics doubt whether anything can be said in general about the nature of art over and above its particular class role and class liaisons. It is, I think, appropriate to discuss these views now, since they raise issues of a rather different nature from those I shall discuss later on. The source of these views lies in the New Left and, as I shall suggest, its protagonists are not typical Marxists. In many ways their views are unorthodox. However if their hypothesis about the nature of art is correct, then any further discussion of its nature would be pointless because there would be nothing to discuss. It is therefore important to consider their arguments before we begin.

The view in question is that art is what we may call a

partisan concept. 'Art' is distinguished by certain over-tones and associations which link it irrevocably with a particular class. The importance of this view lies in the supposed necessity of the connection. If the connection between art and class was claimed to be merely coin-cidental, few would object to the thesis. But a stronger claim is made by some protagonists. It is argued that once stripped of the class associations the concept of art is empty; it has no content left. A quotation may give the flavour of this theory. Roger Taylor's recent book, reveal-ingly entitled *Art an enemy of the people* closes with the line ' "Art" is a value the masses should resist, not just ignore.'[1] Of course, not every writer who is hostile to 'art' and 'culture' takes such an extreme view, though Su Braden borders on it in her book *Artists and People*,

It must be understood that the so-called cultural heritage which made Europe great – the Bachs and Beethovens, the Shakespeares and Dantes, the Constables and Titians – is no longer communicating anything to the vast majority of Europe's population . . . It is bourgeois culture and therefore only immediately meaningful to that group.[2]

Now we may grant that the arts are largely a middle-class preserve. Taylor argues that a concern for the arts is a badge of success in society. Certainly nobody who goes to opera, ballet or to art exhibitions will deny the conten-tion that the vast majority of the patrons belong to the middle classes. This is as true as such sociological generalisations are ever likely to be. Blue-collar workers have their forms of entertainment and they are different from those of the more culturally-aware members of the middle class. This is not, of course, inconsistent with the fact that the great bulk of the middle classes are philis-tines. The point is that where there are patrons of the arts they are unlikely to be working-class people. One reason for this may be that the middle classes traditionally place emphasis on deferred rather than immediate satisfac-tion, and this is supposed not to be a characteristic of blue-collar workers, no doubt for economic reasons. A deep understanding of the arts does demand time and patience. A poem may only become intelligible after many readings and it may take many playings before a piece of music reveals its beauties. Indeed, *contra* Braden, it may well be that the greatest achievements in the arts, the works which may be called 'high art', are not immediately intelligible to anyone at all. They may be more accessible to the bourgeoisie but they are not necessarily immediately intelligible to members of that class.

It needs to be stressed that protagonists of this view have not produced any argument which shows that the class connections of art are other than contingent. It is also worth reminding ourselves of the criticism which artists make explicitly or implicitly of society. Balzac is a good example: although he was a political conservative, the aristocrats he describes seem decrepit rather than admirable. Criticism of their own society by artists is commonplace. The novels of Hardy and the operas of Berg make a powerful plea for the exploited and down-trodden. Mozart's *Marriage of Figaro* was revolutionary because it presents servants as individual human beings of passion and dignity whose needs and emotions are as serious and as deeply felt as those of the aristocrats they served.

The relation of art to society is complex and subtle. As we have seen, artists may bite the hand that feeds them; they may both have a respected and privileged place in society and yet criticise that society. Furthermore, the works of art they produce, though they have their seeds in that society, often have an appeal long after the social conditions in which they are produced have ceased to exist. This has always posed a problem for orthodox Marxism which has simultaneously recognised the complex relation of a creative artist to the society in which he lives and yet has maintained that the under-standing of art derives from an appreciation of its rela-tionship to that society. Because the consciousness of a given era derives from the productive mechanisms at work, the understanding of the art of that era depends upon an understanding of the social forces that made it possible.

Yet Marxists have had to come to terms with the fact that art goes on appealing to people whose knowledge of the historical background is slender. The recognition of the independence of the 'superstructure' does not really help. The culture, ideas and institutions of a society, what Marxists call its 'superstructure', has a measure of independence from its economic base, the system of productive relationships which form the economy. But although this explains the critical role that art may possess, it does not explain the intelligibility of art of the remoter past. Marx was struggling with this when he made his notorious assertion that the appeal of Greek art was to the child in modern man.

The answer to these difficulties may lie in the assumption of a common human nature facing similar stresses and constraints. Such a view is not welcome to Marxists who regard the human condition as the product of society and as variable as the society that creates it. The defence of such a view would require another book and I do not propose to say any more about it here. Suffice that the general criticism of art with which we began is a vulgar and unsophisticated form of Marxism. The more general question it raises will, I trust, be answered in the course of this book. If, by showing that there are general features that art possesses, we neutralise the arguments of those who wish ordinary people to reject art, then the book will not be in vain. For we have removed one bar to the wider appreciation of art, the assumption that it is necessarily a preserve of the wealthier classes. The present situation in which some of the most powerful and profound achievements of mankind are placed beyond the reach of the average man purely through his class self-image is deeply distressing. Providing there is an answer to the question 'what is art?' which goes beyond its class liaisons, we may assume that art is not necessarily alien to the great mass of mankind. Does it all matter? It matters if you believe, as I do, that the appeal and the rewards of great art are deeper, more intense and more lasting. Taylor distinguishes between art and other forms of entertainment purely on the grounds of its class role. There is no other basis for discrimination. I believe that there are grounds for distinction and that as a consequence of these, 'high art' may play a more profound rôle in the development of the identity of its afficionados than the ephemera of popular music and entertainment ever can[3].

2

Classifying the Arts

Although the first contributions to aesthetics were made by the Greeks, notably in Plato's *Ion* and Aristotle's *Poetics*, as a subject the study is fairly recent. The reason is obvious. Until a general conception of the arts developed, as it did in the eighteenth century, there was no place for a philosophical study of the problems of art as a whole; necessarily such a study must attend the development of a general concept.

There are, then, two preliminary questions to be discussed before we turn to a more general examination of the nature of works of art. First, we need to consider how we came to have a general concept of the arts which draws together diverse forms of art such as music, drama, poetry, film and sculpture among others. In part this is a historical question and in part it is a conceptual question, a conceptual question which constitutes the main topic of this book; what makes an artefact a work of art? What do we mean when we describe an object as a work of art? A preliminary to this discussion must be an analysis of the ways in which art can be classified into the literary, visual and performing arts; also it is important to say something initially about the nature of aesthetics as a discipline. So the tasks of this chapter are three-fold. First of all, I shall briefly describe the historical basis for our concept of 'art', secondly, I shall say a little about the origin and nature of the study of aesthetics and finally, at greater length, discuss the classification of the arts. This will lay the groundwork for the subsequent discussion.

The roots of our modern conception of the arts lie in the seventeenth and eighteenth centuries. In a famous pair of papers, Kristeller[1] argued that the modern system of the arts developed through a distinction between those human activities in which progress of the Moderns over the Greeks and Romans can be expected and those where the Moderns show no progress over the Ancients. The first corresponds to what we now call science, the latter to what we now regard as the arts. To a very large measure this distinction holds. We all assume that the sum of human knowledge will steadily increase, especially in the sciences; however the idea that a modern writer can be expected to improve on Shakespeare simply because of the lapse of centuries seems absurd.

Further developments took place in the eighteenth century. First, with the great development in ensemble and instrumental music came the realisation that music too is an independent art, not necessarily subservient to poetry or prose. Instead of being thought of as merely the servant of poetry, setting the words of the poet to music which illustrated the sentiments the poet expressed, music took its place beside poetry as an art in its own right. In time, as we all know, there were debates as to whether film or photography are art forms in their own right. Later we shall consider some of the arguments which can be put forward in favour of regarding film and photography as independent arts, and we shall also discuss the anomalous position of what have been called the 'mixed arts', opera and song, for instance. But there are other features which mitigate against a tidy and orderly taxomony of the arts. Perhaps nothing equals music's capacity to inflict that peculiar brand of ecstasy the French call 'frisson' upon its hearers. On the other hand, literature, music, film or drama may be morally educative, a claim which would sound curious if it were made about music. No doubt this is connected with the fact that censorship is pretty well a constant issue in those arts which we describe as representative, such as the novel, film, drama, painting and verse, whereas the only basis of censorship in music is the idiosyncratic taste of an autocrat. Are music and these other arts 'unequally yoked together' or is there a rationale for classifying them together?

I shall argue later in this book that although the notion of an art may be something of a rag-bag and various independent historical factors may have produced the collection of various arts which we currently have, there are certain pervasive elements in these differing arts. An art contains a conscious tradition in which earlier works are related to later. *Cognoscenti* can 'place' a painting or a poem or piece of music to within a decade or so on stylistic grounds. Secondly, works of art are objects for interpretation. I shall elaborate upon these two notions which I believe to be both fundamental in aesthetics and internal to the concept of art in later chapters.

The word 'aesthetics' we owe to a German philosopher, Baumgarten (1714-62), who adapted it from the Greek word which means 'to perceive'. Asthetics he described as the science of sensory awareness. Aesthetics become heir to a long philosophical tradition of interest in the idea of beauty. One twist given this tradition by post-Rennaissance thought was to treat beauty as the pre-dominant characteristic of works of art so that it was in contemplating works of art that we preeminently appre-hend beauty. As Dickie observes,[2] this has not been all for the good. The spiritual overtones to be found in Plotinus's writings on beauty and which are probably implicit in Plato's Theory of Forms have led to a rather pompous attitude to art, summarised in that absurd and embarrassing couplet by Keats about truth and beauty. Dickie properly remarks that works of art can be funny, witty and gay as well.

By the mid-nineteenth century 'aesthetics' had be-come generally accepted as the common noun referring to the study of the philosophical problems arising out of the existence of the arts. At this point we need to make a distinction which this definition obfuscates. We obtain aesthetic pleasure from a great variety of objects and activities. It is not merely playing and listening to music, reading verse, or going to a play that gives aesthetic pleasure. People get aesthetic stimulation from watching football or cricket; how else does one imagine that strokes or moves are graded? It is not merely strength and success which we admire in the gifted sportsman. A move at chess or a mathematical proof may be elegant or beautiful. So may gardens, landscapes, townscapes, coffee cups, animals, birds, men or women, cars or aircraft. None of these are works of art. Indeed the aesthetic aspect of life is so marked that it hardly seems an exaggeration to speak of man as the aesthetic animal.

Conversely, not only do objects other than works of art give aesthetic pleasure, but on a quite intuitively plausible definition of aesthetic pleasure we may judge that many works of art may not give aesthetic pleasure. If one thinks of aesthetic pleasure as paradigmatically the sort of occasion when you suddenly stop and catch your breath at a Lakeland view or at Gower's cover drive then it needs to be pointed out that many works of art can be profoundly affecting without giving that sort of frisson. One might very well read right through Middlemarch or Bleak House without feeling anything like that at all; these novels move us by engaging our sympathy for their characters; to be deeply affected by Mr Bulstrode's tears at his humiliation before his wife is not aesthetic pleasure: yet we may close the book with a sense of astonishment at George Eliot's achievement much as we may feel in the presence of music that makes us ecstatic. So aesthetic pleasure and a genuine and appropriate response to a work of art are not identical although they do overlap. Once pointed out this seems obvious enough but it is a sufficiently widespread confusion to have been damaging. As a result the study of aesthetics had been in part misplaced and in part unduly restricted.

In fact, recent work in aesthetics has been sufficiently interesting and sufficiently analytic in tone to merit an improvement in its status. It does not deserve to be the Cinderella of philosophy and its reputation as such is no longer deserved. The revolutionary work of Wittgenstein and Ryle, amongst others, in the philosophy of mind has had its effect upon aesthetics in its repercussions on the study of such important concepts as expression, emotion and intention; recent work on the philosophy of language has also created eddies in aesthetics. Consequently the subject has increased very considerably in vitality since the early fifties when J.A. Passmore could, with justification, entitle a paper 'The Dreariness of Aesthetics'.

One familiar definition of aesthetics is that it studies the philosophical problems which arise from the existence of beautiful objects and their contemplation by men. This seems to presuppose that objects of aesthetic admiration are objects of beauty. This proposition does not in turn presuppose that aesthetic admiration can only be directed at works of art for some objects of beauty are not works of art; nevertheless the definition remains far too narrow and as an attempt to record the content of the concept of the aesthetic it fails to survive the most cursory examination. Are *King Lear*, *The Rite of Spring*, or Goya's etchings of summary executions things of beauty? Art is both greater and more various.

Indeed, as early as the eighteenth century Burke attempted to classify art and objects of aesthetic attention; some were sublime, some beautiful, others graceful and yet others elegant. (The contrast between the beautiful and sublime was, of course, widely recognised.) The concept of sublimity received much attention: a sublime vista connoted danger to the traveller; a sublime work of art transported its listener or reader. The term remains in vogue to this day as the highest praise which can be accorded to a work of art. Only the very greatest works are sublime; for example, Bach's *B Minor Mass*, *King Lear* or the self-portraits of Rembrandt's later years. A graceful work of art displays economy of form, but carries as well the suggestion of smallness of scale. A Strauss waltz might be graceful but not a Beethoven symphony, a lyric by Herrick but not a sonnet by Donne.

This classification is not without its value and would benefit from the attentions of a modern analytic philosopher; however much it needs improvement, it does in its present unreformed state at least suggest the conclusion that objects of beauty are not the sole targets of aesthetic discussion and appraisal. To describe aesthetics as the theory of beauty is at least to place an impediment in the course of subsequent enquiry.

A suggestion that attracts many modern philosophers comes from Professor M.C. Beardsley.[3] He proposes that aesthetics be defined as the study of problems which arise from the criticism of the arts. It is because critics make judgements, offer reasons for their judgements and interpret works of art that aesthetics exists. For we then find ourselves asking whether the sorts of reason they offer support the conclusions they draw. In a word aesthetics is metacriticism. It talks about critical talk.

As a field of study, aesthetics consists of a rather hetero-geneous collection of problems: those that arise when we make a serious effort to say something true and warranted about a work of art. As a field of knowledge, aesthetics consists of those principles that are required for clarifying and confirm-ing critical statements. Aesthetics can be thought of, then, as the philosophy of criticism, or *metacriticism (original italics)*.

Now unquestionably there are many problems in aes-thetics which occur because of the judgements that critics make. I have listed a couple and, in the passage quoted, Beardsley offers some more. But I would main-tain that many of the problems of aesthetics do not seem to be as closely related to the existence of critical dis-course as this. For example, there are problems to do with the classification of the arts, problems which I discuss later in this chapter. Music and drama are per-forming arts and the ontological status of the works themselves is by no means clear. We might argue with some plausibility that there is a sense in which we cannot encounter Beethoven's Seventh Symphony *per se*: we only encounter a performance of it or read the score. On the other hand, there is also some plausibility in saying that we encounter it every time we hear a performance Whatever we decide it is proper to say in these cases, the situation is obviously very different from that which obtains in the visual arts. I can see the actual Mona Lisa, but only if I visit the Louvre. We wish to say that the work of art is identical with a physical object in that it is wherever the physical object is and that when that object ceases to exist the work of art ceases to exist. Suffice for the present that such questions do not relate in the same way to the existence of critical discussion as do questions about critical standards and critical interpretation. I prefer to make a tripartite distinction between the various sorts of questions which make up the subject matter of aesthetics.

1   Questions of ontology. (What is the nature of a work of art? What is the difference between the work and a copy? How do performances relate to the work?)
2   Questions of phenomenology. (What is the nature of our reaction to works of art? How do they affect us?)
3   Questions about judgement. (What sort of judgements are judgements of value and critical interpretations of works of art? How do we support them by the reasons we offer?)

These questions may overlap, and sometimes answers to one group have been construed or perhaps misconstrued as answers to another, but as a rough and ready preliminary distinction will serve to dictate the order of our discussions.

I have mentioned the fact that a painting is identical with a physical object. If you wish to see the Mona Lisa then you must visit the Louvre. There are, of course, copies and photographs and from these you may get a pretty fair idea of the original. It is also true that we say things of the object *qua* painting which might seem odd said of the physical object *simpliciter*: a still life may be described as having depth, for example, whereas the physical object is flat. But my earlier point remains the crucial one: destroy the object and you destroy the work of art. (The 'depth' of a still life must be regarded as metaphorical, I think. We can say that the Mona Lisa has depth and a Mondrian has not, without wishing to deny that both are flat when contrasted with a relief.) But you have not seen the Mona Lisa unless and until you have seen the object which hangs in Paris. In this respect painting and sculpture are quite unlike other arts; if asked whether I have read *Middle-march* I do not hesitate because I have not read George Eliot's autograph. The point is that the physical marks made by the creator are aesthetically relevant in the first case, whereas they are not in the second. I may know very thoroughly what the Mona Lisa looks like, but it would be unwise of me to trust my judgement about its relative aesthetic merits or any judgement of an inter- pretative nature, about for example its relation to earlier Italian art or about the point of the indeterminate execu- tion of the landscape, until I have actually seen it. Once I have seen it I may still fail to notice many important things about it, and I am as liable to misjudgement as the next man through my relative ignorance of painting of that period or my inexperience in making judgements. But one crucially important barrier to a sound opinion has been removed. I have seen the Mona Lisa and not just a copy. It is in some ways like, though of course also in many ways unlike, reading a novel as against seeing the film or reading a potted version. No parallel barrier remains to be removed once I have read *Middlemarch* unabridged. The first condition for judging and discus- sing has been met even if my equipment as a critic is miserably inadequate. Admittedly, even in the case of paintings and sculpture, the identity between the work of art and the physical object is not unproblematic and some thinkers make a sharp distinction between the two. A Renaissance painting of a figure may show the figure clad in a crimson cloak which has turned brown with age. *Qua* aesthetic object, it is sometimes argued, the cloak is crimson, but *qua* physical object the cloak is brown. The painting is expressive of religious devotion but the col- lection of pigments is not. My inclination is to side-step this issue by distinguishing the aesthetic properties from the non-aesthetic properties of a single object; the same object may then be individuated by either the one group of properties or the other.

Now philosophers make the distinction between the two sorts of art in various ways. One is to employ the distinction between type and token introduced by the great American philosopher, Charles Sanders Peirce.[4]

A common mode of estimating the amount of matter in a MS. or printed book is to count the number of words. There will ordinarily be about twenty *the*'s on a page, and of course they count as twenty words. In another sense of the word 'word', however, there is but one word 'the' in the English language; and it is impossible that this word should lie visibly on a page or be heard in any voice, for the reason that it is not a Single thing or Single event. It does not exist; it only determines things that do exist. Such a definitely significant Form, I propose to term a *Type*. A Single event which happens once and whose identity is limited to that one happening or a Single object or thing which is in some single place at any one instant of time, such event or thing being significant only as occurring just when and where it does, such as this or that word on a single line of a single page of a single copy of a book, I will venture to call a *Token*.

This distinction is not the same as the distinction between a universal and instances of that universal. In part we can see this in the way we speak about universals on the one hand and types on the other. We may say that this pillar box exemplifies the universal 'redness' but we do not say that this token pillar box exemplifies the type 'pillar box'. A patch of colour may exemplify the universal redness but is not a type of that token. More significantly a type and its token share many properties. If the Union Jack is *qua* type rectangular then any token of it is rectangular. If the type consists of a pattern created by the superimposition of crosses then the token consists of a pattern created by the superimposition of crosses. But whereas we can say of both type and token that they possess these common properties we cannot speak in the same way of the universal and its exemplifying cases. The patch of colour which exemplifies redness will necessarily be red, but the universal is not itself red, it is simply redness.

Equally the relation between type and token is not the relation between class and member. What properties class and member possess in common is fortuitous; they might both be large for example. But the type and the token of that type share all necessary and individuating properties. The type and the token of the red flag share their colour and shape of necessity. But the class of Red Indians does not possess the properties which make us count a particular man as a Red Indian. The class is not rational, red-skinned and descended from the earlier inhabitants of America.

Finally, as has recently been pointed out, we can create types but not universals. Somebody invented the Union Jack; Shakespeare wrote *Coriolanus*. Once the first token has been produced then subsequent tokens can be made of that type. It does not however follow that the creation of the type is necessarily contemporaneous with the creation of the first token. An inventor might merely leave the blueprint for a type and somebody else produce the first token.

The distinction between type and token, as expressed in the quotation from Peirce, is not entirely clear but he evidently has in mind the distinction between 'the' viewed as an object existing neither in time nor space and the word 'the' as it appears on this page and elsewhere. It is true of the type that it has three letters, is the definite article in English, but not that it is printed or written anywhere in particular. What are written or printed at particular times and places are tokens of that type.

The topic properly belongs to the province of philosophical logic; all that we require is a clarity relative to the job to be done and it is not hard to see how the distinction may be applied to works of literature. There is no particular physical object which is identical with the sonnet 'Shall I Compare Thee to a Summer's Day?'; there are no physical marks left by the author without acquaintance with which the reader is less adequately prepared for the task of understanding and enjoying the poem. At the very least this is the common assumption and anybody who maintained that a full understanding of the poem demanded a familiarity with the autograph would need to make out a case for it. Literature would then begin to converge on calligraphy. As things stand the poem is a type and of this type the copies are tokens. The creation of the first token might have been simultaneous with the creation of the type if Shakespeare composed it as he wrote rather than composing it in his head, only writing it down later. It is, however, but a token, and if the autograph is lost the work is not lost. Even if all tokens were destroyed by some Philistine tyrant, the poem would continue to exist as long as some readers could recite it from memory. Some readers may remember the moving conclusion to Truffaut's film of Bradbury's *Fahrenheit 451* where refugees from a society which burns books live a precarious existence in nearby forests. Each has memorised a classic which they can recite to their fellows and they have become known by the titles of the books they remember.

The type token distinction seems to me to fit tolerably well the relation between a film and its prints or a photograph and its prints as well as the relation between a work of literature and its printed or written copies. But whether it fits the relation between a piece of music or a play and its performance seems to me much more debatable. Several writers have claimed that the relation between work and performance is a type-token relationship. Wollheim, for example, treats works of music and works of literature on a par. '*Ulysses* and *Der Rosenkavalier* are types; my copy of *Ulysses* and tonight's performance of *Rosenkavalier* are tokens of those types.' Certainly in each of these cases we can attribute features to the putative token which the putative type cannot possess. A performance of *Rosenkavalier* takes place at a particular opera house at a particular time; my copy of *Ulysses* is currently to be found on the top shelf in my study. But *qua* works of art neither exists at any particular place or time: they are abstract objects with which particular tokens comply.

But performances can be quite plausibly regarded as tokens of a type other than the work. A conductor or a pianist creates an interpretation of a piece of music which he then performs, possibly many times. If he is a well-known artist then his interpretation may become well-known. Musicians speak of 'Klemperer's *Eroica*', Toscanini's *Seventh*.' Guilini's Verdi *Requiem*' or 'Solo-

mon's *Hammerklavier'* as particularly celebrated interpretations. They become familiar and well loved and
may be performed again and again, and probably recorded. Peter Brook's *A Midsummer Night's Dream* was
a famous theatrical production which embodied that
director's interpretation of the work, and which was then
performed again and again and subsequently filmed. The
performances are, indeed, tokens of that particular type
where the type is the interpretation. The interpretation
may change over time. Musicians examine with interest
the changes in Karajan's conception of Beethoven over
the last three decades, for he has recorded several
complete sets of the Beethoven symphonies. Some interpreters seem to approach the work afresh on each occasion they publically perform it and there is little
consistency amongst their various interpretations.
Others – less 'spontaneous artists' as the critical jargon
goes – prepare an interpretation very carefully and only
change it after much thought. It is also very striking that
critics tend to judge interpretations much as they judge
works of art themselves. They admire originality and
coherence in the interpretation. A pianist is said to 'make
every note count' much as we say of a great poem that
every word is necessary to the effect of the whole and
that to amend a single line would be damaging. Equally it
is true that there are traditions of interpretation which the
great performer may revolutionise. I read recently that
Debussy's *Jeux* has been rarely performed and that
there is therefore no performing tradition which helps the
conductor find his bearings. On the other hand there are
sometimes traditions so strong that they form a strait-
jacket. Spike Hughes said of Toscanini:

Toscanini gave a characteristically literal performance of the
Pathétique, removed all the dust and dirt and the over painting
of bathos and vulgarity that the work had accumulated over
the years and restored an old masterpiece to all its original
brilliant and spontaneous colour.[5]

I think we should resist the implication that Toscanini
somehow presented Tchaikovski's symphony as it is in

itself, the very *ding-an-sich*, free from any tincture of his own personality. A Toscanini performance can usually be recognised as such by an experienced musician for a great interpreter's personality inevitably colours the work. It is of the nature of a performing art that this should be so. The point is that Toscanini changed interpretative traditions by his emphasis on clearer and more direct performances of the standard repertoire. Parallel considerations apply, of course, in the theatre: Gielgud, Olivier, Guinness,Redgrave and Warner, amongst others, have something different to say about the playing of Hamlet and their interpretations modify the traditional picture or pictures of the role handed down to them by virtue of thier own theatrical experience and personality. It is worth noting as well that a copy of an interpretation has the same status as a copy of a work of art. A child prodigy who produces his teacher's interpretation of a work, albeit with the utmost panache, produces but a copy of that interpretation and not an interpretation in its own right, much as a copy of a painting is not a work of art but merely a copy of one.

I think we can begin to see the ways in which literary tokens and tokens in the performing arts differ. It matters not a jot whether I read *Ulysses* in hardback or paperback providing the print is legible. No literary considerations arise. The only aesthetic questions possible are questions about the appearance of the book. Consequently it does not matter if I begin with the paperback and end with the hardback. But although I may get a reasonably clear idea of the notes if I listen to half Klemperer's recording of Mahler's *Das Lied* and end with Bruno Walter's, something important has been lost. I have lost the opportunity to experience either great conductor's view of the work. If he regards the last song as the climax he will interpret the other movements accordingly. If he regards the last song as an extended coda to a symphonic argument which has occupied the earlier movements then we must expect a less weighty view of the *Abschied*. In either case we have lost the coherence that a single interpretation gives us. We have no consistent impression of either view of the work. Furthermore we cannot regard the performance as a single performance. It is but two parts of two different performances juxtaposed. It is thus not a single token of the type.

My suggestion is then that we regard the token as the performance and the type as the interpretation and that we therefore distinguish the performing arts from works of literature where the token is the individual copy and the work the type. If it were the custom to read poetry aloud more often than it is read at present, and if silent private reading of poetry were regarded as a substitute for the genuine thing, much as the reading of a score is regarded as a substitute for actually hearing the work performed, then, presumably, poetry would converge on the other performing arts and parallel distinctions between work, interpretation and performance would hold. Then we could look forward to hearing Ted Hughes' interpretation of his own poetry much as we are interested in Tippet's interpretation of his own music. But as long as novel reading and poetry reading is normally private, there is a case for a distinction between the performing arts and literature.

What confers identity upon a token performance is not that the same work is being performed throughout, but that a single interpretation is being performed throughout. How then do we regard the score? The best analogy is to think of it as we think of a recipe. Just as a cook produces a cake by means of the recipe yet still adds his own touch to the finished product, so the interpreter takes the score as a recipe for the performance. The score, however, under-determines the interpretation. How fast is *andante con moto*, just how loud is *mf*? It is in the gap between what the notation specifies and what the performance contains that the great interpreter shows his mettle. There will always be critics to be found who believe that the necessary latitude allowed the interpreter through the lack of specificity in the notation is sufficient for the great interpreter to create a conception of the work that, like works of art proper, both relates to a tradition of interpretation and adds to it. As against this it is an observable fact that some great interpreters depart from the letter of the notation with results that *cognoscenti* applaud.

Nelson Goodman, in *Languages of Art*, proposes a different basis for the classification of the arts. In music, he points out, there is no such thing as a forgery of a known work whereas there can, of course, be a forgery of a known work in painting. There is a familiar and no doubt apocryphal story of a Texan visiting an English country house and, in seeing a Gainsborough, remarking 'I have the original at home'. There is no parallel to forgery of this sort in music. Nobody could pass off a copy of the *London Symphony* though they might try to pass off a forged autograph. Indeed the contrast between genuine and forged does not hold with respect to printed or written copies. There can, of course, be works passed off as by Haydn which are not by Haydn at all; this was, indeed a flourishing cottage industry once he became famous, but that is another matter.[6]

Goodman calls a work autographic if the distinction between the original and a forgery is significant, and allographic if it is not. Thus painting and sculpture are autographic, music, literature, photography and film are allographic. It is with respect to allographic works that we raised the question of how the type-token distinction applies.

The distinction arises out of an interesting question which may as well be dealt with here as elsewhere. It is about the status and aesthetic merit of fakes. Non-specialists are inclined to argue that if the experts are taken in by a fake then the fake ought to be accorded the same value as the original. Now there are two cases here which need to be distinguished: there are forgeries which purport to be a particular known painting by the master in question. There could be a forged Mona Lisa and there are apparently forgeries of known paintings by Gainsborough. On the other hand there are fakes which merely purport to be by a certain master; they are presented as lost or hitherto unknown works. The most famous fakes fall into this category; for instance the

Vermeer forgeries of van Meegeren and the Samuel Palmer forgeries of Keating. So does it matter if van Meegeren produces a Vemeer-type painting three centuries after the death of the latter and deceives the experts? Those who reply in the negative normally do so because they regard the relations between the artist and the work as aesthetically contingent; in their view it matters not a whit how and when and by whom a picture was painted; what matters is the picture and how we respond to it. In literature this attitude finds expression in the anti-intentionalism of the New Criticism and, even more, in the idea of Practical Criticism. Undergraduates studying English literature are, even now, confronted with a poem or a slice of prose which they are then invited to 'evaluate'. The assumption is that a poem, like other works of art, can be understood, at least as far as its essential properties are concerned, in ignorance of its provenance and the historical environment which gave it birth. It is not hard to see the strength in this view; knowing that a painting was by a great master may make us approach it with a reverence it does not deserve. On the other hand, it is surely a condition of understanding a work of art that we endeavour to appreciate its originality, its relation to its predecessors in that tradition, and its place in an *oeuvre*. Is the rhyme scheme in this poem merely conventional? To know whether it is or not requires knowing at what period it was written. Heroic couplets may have been conventional in Augustan verse but they are not so today. If this is written in heroic couplets and belongs to the Augustan era then we may keep an eye open for minute variations of the convention. If not, then we may identify an element of pastiche in the poem set there for a particular effect. Consider, for example, the use of pastiche in Eliot's *Four Quartets*. Again, if the poem predates the Augustan period then we may think of it as anticipatory and original in that way.

It would be idle to deny that the reader approaches verse with tacit knowledge of this sort. Even the most ignorant undergraduate knows something of the development of literary style and diction in English literature and, consciously or unconsciously, he will place a poem by those features. Most practised readers or listeners will date a poem or piece of music within a decade or so and it is only the very occasional case which throws them. So that what is offered as Practical Criticism is nothing of the sort if by that is meant the examination of the work in *eo ipso*.

The way in which such knowledge is applied varies. In literature it can be extremely important because it determines the sense we give to the words. We all know how words like 'nice' and 'presently' have changed in a few centuries. The epigraph to John Wain's *Hurry on Down* contains a quotation from Wordsworth, 'Heaven look down on this poor sod'; the joke depends upon an ambiguity in 'sod' which has arisen since the writing of the poem. Then again, as I have argued, we may need to know the conventions of iconography and symbolism of the time in order to read off the significance of emblems. This holds equally in painting. One cannot begin to understand Giorgione without an understanding of his iconography, and one does not know that iconography is relevant until one knows when the painting was produced. Equally, to know when a piece of music was written is to be equipped to decide whether a certain device is a cliché or a novelty. So our net impression of the work, what Ingarden calls our 'concretion', is dependent on our estimate of the place of that work in the history of the art. One other way in which this surfaces is in the way certain features of the work appear as foreground and others as background. Experienced listeners look for the first and second subjects of a sonata form movement and these themes project in their hearing of the music, relegating bridge passages to background.

How then does this relate to the question of forgery? A forgery deliberately gives the public a false historical perspective. Suppose, on seeing a van Meegeren, we pick out a certain feature in the painting as being original; so it might have been had it been painted in the sixteenth century; but, being painted in the thirties, it is part of the repertoire of the least competent artist. Again, had it been painted in the time of Vermeer its relation to religious ideas would have been necessarily different from the relation which a painting of the 1930s has. Forgeries stand to genuine art as lies stand to truth telling. They are parasites. They need the existence of genuine art for the idea of a continuing historical tradition of works: works in this tradition depend upon their predecessors and at the same time vary the repertoire of devices available. Genuine works of art attempt to continue and surmount the tradition. 'Aufgeheben' is the untranslatable German word for the relation. But forgeries steal a place in that tradition by pretending to an achievement which is, *au fond*, the right of their predecessors. The point is made quite admirably by Mark Roskill.[7]

A forger is cashing in our knowledge of the history of art. By giving us false information about the painting's date he leads us to apply false standards and make false assumptions, for we can never look at a painting totally objectively. A forger is pretending to an originality that he does not possess. He is dishonouring the very aspects of a great artist's originality which make that artist's work live from century to century (p.167).

(Incidentally, the awfulness of van Meegeren's paintings makes it hardly credible that anybody should have been deceived. Roskill suggests that it is the clichés of the thirties, so apparent to us now, which make it clear when they were produced. But these clichés could not have been so clear to the artists and public of the time. Unnoticed, they allowed the public to see similarities with Vermeer which now evade us. On the other hand, it also has to be said that some critics who did see them instantly pronounced them to be fakes. Keating's Palmers look more competent jobs to us, though, of course, they may not look so in a quarter of a century when the clichés of the seventies have been left behind.)

Those who defend Keating and van Meegeren, who take at face value Keating's charge that he simply sought to *épater les bourgeois*, treat works of art as though, like the beauty of a virgin forest, their aesthetic qualities have no necessary connection with any human institutions or society. But art is not like this; it is a human product which bears an intimate relationship to the society which produced it.

The second type of forgery returns us to the questions which occupied us earlier in this chapter. Forgers sometimes pass a copy off as an original. A forger might copy a Rembrandt and sell the forgery to an unsuspecting millionaire as the original Rembrandt. To circumvent both kinds of forgery art dealers employ experts to validate a work, determining that its provenance is as is claimed. The interesting evaluative question is now whether, if a painting is such an excellent copy of an original that no expert can tell which one is genuine even when they are placed side by side, we should conclude that they have the same aesthetic value. They will not, presumably, have the same financial value; nobody imagines that collectors are motivated only by aesthetic interests. But as far as the critic is concerned he might as well attend to the forgery as to the original. Goodman argues against the antecedent of this conditional on the grounds that there can be no way of excluding the possibility that somebody might observe some difference between the two. This is no doubt the case in the present state of reproduction in which we are dependent either upon colour photography or the work of another artist. If, however, some new process develops where the reproduction can be guaranteed to be an exact replica of the original, through the existence of causal connections of a law-like sort, might matters be different? It would always be open for a sceptic to decry the reproduction on the grounds that the law-like connection was not proven watertight and that consequently some observer might eventually discover some difference. But if experts were normally unable to detect any difference between the two, we might conclude that for aesthetic purposes there was no way of telling them apart. One can then imagine it to be but a short step to the defining of aesthetically relevant properties in such a way that a necessary condition for x being an aesthetically relevant feature of a painting is that the painting shares it with all other copies of the original obtained by the process in question. If this happened then the original would be causally significant in the production of the other tokens of the type just as the poet's autograph is causally significant in that from it the other copies are generated. If x is a copy of a copy then the process eventually leads back to the original which is a copy of nothing else. But that apart there would be no special reason to mark out the original. In other words it would be a token of a type amongst other tokens of a type. In part then it is a question of a decision as to whether to regard the visual arts as exhibiting type-token relationships, or whether here and here alone the work of art is identical with a physical object. It is not entirely a matter of a decision because we presume that a certain technological level is required before the former becomes a possibility.

In sum, then, the type-token distinction seems to me as useful a way to distinguish the various arts as any other currently available and it has the virtue of providing a conceptual vocabulary in which certain philosophical problems about the interrelations of works and their interpretation and performance and various aesthetic issues concerning the nature of forgery can be raised. However it must be clear that the ontological distinctions made are dependent upon certain contingencies concerning the way we regard art. I mentioned the fact that poetry is no longer normally thought of as having to be read aloud, for example. If it were once again regarded as necessary to read it aloud, it would become a performing art. Perhaps if music lovers became more adept at score reading, music might move in the opposite direction.

There are, as well, arts which appear not to fall clearly into the category of either music or drama. Opera is, of course, the obvious example. The critical listener to opera looks for the way in which the singer not only casts the vocal line but relates it to the words he sings. So the music must be projected with an eye to its structural relation to the music as a whole, and with respect to the meaning of the words set. But so much is also true of *lieder*, of course. In addition, the opera singer and conductor have to take into account the dramatic aspect of the music. Opera is, as Joseph Kerman averred, *drama per musica*. So the Wagnerian conception of music drama has much to recommend it, though of course far from beginning with him the principles are evident in Mozart as well as earlier opera composers. So there are arguments which favour Beardsley's claim that song is a 'mixed art' and the same arguments favour treating opera as mixed art. The arguments I have presented depend essentially on the assumption that different critical approaches are brought into play. If the voice is treated as an instrument, as in the wordless chorus which closes Holst's *Planets*, then the critical approach to the use of those voices is no different from that required when we listen to instrumental music *simpliciter*. But when the words matter then the critic has to assess how both composer and singer make the music reflect and underscore the words. These considerations are not purely musical. Not only does this principle require that we consider opera a mixed art but ballet too must be classified as a mixed art. The use of sets and the way they are designed so as to integrate into the interpretation as a whole is a factor the critic will consider.

What about film? Is this a mixed art, or an art in its own right? We shall consider later the thesis that film is merely photographed dramatic performance. This I find unacceptable. It seems to me that the considerations required of the critic, the range of techniques available, and their peculiarity to the film, make an unanswerable case for regarding film neither as a mixed art nor as a filmed dramatic performance but as an art *per se.*

3

What Art is!

We began by considering some attempts to classify the arts, and we eventually concluded that the type-token distinction offered a reasonably adequate basis for distinguishing the various arts. The natural sequel is to consider why we classify these diverse forms as 'art'. What is it that makes an artefact a work of art? In setting this question I have already hinted at part of the answer in the very formulation, since I imply that a work of art is an artefact, something made by a person. On the whole, few philosophers will object to that assumption. There are some borderline cases such as *objets trouvés* but these are precisely borderline cases because we are not certain whether something which is merely selected by an artist counts, by that very process, as something the artist has created. I would be inclined to argue that an *objet trouvé*, a curiously shaped piece of driftwood or pleasingly formed rock, has simply the aesthetic attraction that many natural objects have, and that its aesthetic features are of the same order as the aesthetic features of a landscape unshaped by man. It is not a work of art until the artist does something to it beyond just picking it out.

Our question is, then, what makes some artefacts works of art? What do these various objects have in common? We shall consider some answers; these vary from the proposition that artefacts are works of art in virtue of their expressing something about their creator, to the suggestion that there is no one thing that works of art have in common but that they rather compose a family of objects which have no common property.

NEO-WITTGENSTEINIAN THEORIES

It may be as well to begin wih the latter proposal. The suggestion is that works of art are rather like games. It is difficult, if not impossible, as Wittgenstein memorably pointed out, to find a single feature which makes a game a game. Is there a distinction between victor and vanquished? This holds for very many games, of course, but not for a game like Patience or a child's game of throwing a ball against a wall. Sometimes luck and sometimes skill have the larger part. Wittgenstein writes[1]:

67. I can think of no better expression to characterise these similarities than 'family resemblances'; for the various resemblances between members of a family: build, feature, colour of eyes, gait, temperament etc. etc. overlap and criss-cross in the same way — And I shall say: 'games' form a family.

'Family' is not a particularly pellucid term here. The members of a family have a defining condition over and above their resemblances in virtue of which they all belong to the family; they are bound by blood or marriage. But a game, it may be argued, is a particularly appropriate analogy for art. The various groups of works which form the class of works of art may not have any single defining characteristic. Some are representational arts, like drama, the novel and the visual arts, whilst others, like music and architecture, are not. Some are temporal arts in that the form in which we encounter them precludes our returning to an earlier part at a later stage; thus music is heard at a single sitting and once a bar has passed it cannot be brought back to be inspected again in that performance. On the other hand although reading a novel is also a linear process there is nothing to stop us returning to an earlier section to check upon a point. Seeing a picture, though it takes time, is not a linear process in the way that hearing music or reading literature is. There is no prescribed order in which we must view the picture, starting say at the top left and working down and across. Again some works of art are identical with physical objects; some not. Some of these differences relate to those we recounted in the previous chapter. Others are new. Together they make up a case for regarding the arts as a Wittgensteinian 'family'. Another reason sometimes put forward for regarding art as having no single defining condition is that art is quintessentially creative and that any definition taken seriously by the art-world is likely to confine 'art' to a degree which would hamper future artists. But the plausibility of this last criticism rests upon the assumption that an analysis of 'work of art' is bound to be unsuccessful; for, *per impossible*, a satisfactory analysis would permit the production of novel art without contravening the rubric of the analysis. We ought not, however, to be unduly defeatist about the possibility of a satisfactory analysis and with this in mind, I propose to set aside the neo-Wittgensteinian family resemblance theory until we have exhausted alternative analyses. It strikes me as very much a theory to be adopted *faute de mieux*; it may have to be accepted but we may hope that the necessity will not arise.

Indeed, the main reason why this form of theory came to have such an appeal was a general belief that attempts to present the nature of art in the form of a definition had failed. What was wrong, it was surmised, was not that so far we had failed to get the right answer through lack of diligence or looking in the right place. What was wrong was the very enterprise; the mistake lay in the assumption that the arts had a common nature or an essence at all. At the time of writing the climate of philosophical opinion has swung back in favour of some form of essentialism and neo-Wittgensteinism is no longer so influential. It is vulnerable to the single counter example, though the counter example itself may be very hard to find. The counter example in question is, of course, a satisfactory analysis of the concept of art. In specifying the unique form which interpretation takes in the arts I hope to lay the ground for such a general theory of the arts and the Epilogue summarises my conclusions. Consequently I do not think that the neo-Wittgensteinian account needs to be accepted and I do not propose to spend any more time on it.

As respects innovation it is in the invention shown in particular works of art that originality is most often manifested; perhaps we should distinguish between the novelty shown in creating new genres and the novelty shown in creating works of art within a genre. A restrictive definition of art would, I think, more probably restrain the development of new genres such as film than the creation of new works within an existing genre. It is only likely to affect the latter where very new techniques are being adopted. It is in such cases as the works of Cage or Stockhausen that we begin to wonder whether what is being produced counts as music or not.

ART WORLD THEORIES

It is precisely phenomena of this last sort which has in a large part brought about one of the most interesting of recent theories about art, the art world theory. John Cage's silent music is a well-known example of such 'music'; the pianist sits at the piano for 4 minutes 33 seconds (the title of the piece) and does not play a note; the music lies in whatever sounds happen to occur during the period; the audience may cough, retch, leave, rustle sweet papers and probably laugh. Other forms of music are created by the random tuning of radios to short wave frequencies and static. Yet another example is scored as follows; a line is tied from one side of the auditorium to the other. The performers are on one side and the audience on the other; the work commences as performers place objects, clothing for instance, on the string. At any time members of the audience can move across to join the performers or vice versa. The performance ends when the string breaks or when it can take no more objects. (*En passant*, it is hard to see why this should count as a piece of music rather than a dramatic performance or as visual art.)

In the visual arts we have works like Duchamps celebrated 'Fountain', (an inverted urinal signed 'R. Mutt') and other 'ready-mades' such as bottle-racks. It is a sign of the times that a recent newspaper report described how cleaners at the Haywood gallery explained their reluctance to remove some plastic sacks containing rubbish; the grounds they gave were that the sacks might have been works of art. Poetry has been produced which consists of blank pages, and novels with chapters which can be shuffled by the reader to produce a plot to his own satisfaction.

Theorists are reluctant to deny that these count as art; in part their pusillanimity derives from a healthy recognition of the bad press originally given to musicians, writers and painters who are now acknowledged masters. The early experiences of Stravinsky and Schoenberg are etched deeply upon the mind of the contemporary music critic. If, however, we are prepared to recognise these as art even while conceding that they are not particularly good or successful art, then we need a conception of art which is relatively permissive.

Such a conception is provided in the 'art world' or 'institutional' account of what it is to be a work of art. Several writers have advocated a theory of this character, but it has become most closely associated with George Dickie. Dickie's initial move is to draw a sharp distinction between a descriptive and an evaluative sense of 'work of art'. The evaluative sense is seen in the way we sometimes admiringly say of an object 'That's a real work of art'. Often we speak this way, however, about objects which we would not normally count as works of art in their own right. It would be a curious way of announcing one's admiration for a Rembrandt, for example, but not of expressing pleasure in a book-jacket, a speech or a pop song which lifts itself above the customarily mediocre level. So there is an element of suspicion about the appropriateness of the distinction. In normal contexts the evaluative use seems more like hyperbole.

Another possible criticism which might be levelled is that this distinction misrepresents the way in which the concept of art operates. What we have is not a descriptive sense in which the concept has reasonably clear boundaries; 'art' is not a concept comparable with the concept of 'furniture' or the concept of an 'aircraft'. We have instead certain paradigms as to what sorts of artefact are works of art. Clearly a Shakespeare play or a Rembrandt or a Beethoven quartet are works of art. Around these are ranged large numbers of fairly central cases, but also a number of borderline cases such as those examples with which I began this section: the concept is then a concept with extremely fuzzy boundaries.

I think this is probably true. The concept of art is not a precisely drawn concept; however we may grant this without concluding that there can be no adequate analysis of the core of the concept. It is just such an analysis that Dickie offers.[2] Dickie argues that what decides that an artefact should count as a work of art is the say-so of the art world. It is essentially an account of art in terms of a certain social institution, namely the institution of the art world. The art world comprises the world of impresarios, gallery owners, publishers, editors, dealers and critics as well as poets, painters and musicians. It comprises those who are genuinely and seriously concerned with the arts. They and they alone are empowered to 'christen' artefacts works of art and it is by their imprimatur that artefacts become works of art.

Not everything in the object as presented counts as part of the work. The conductor's taps on his desk are not the very beginning of the piece of music. The frame is not part of the picture nor the proscenium arch part of the theatrical set. There are thus certain conventions transmitted with the tradition to which the work belongs which determine what belongs to the work of art and what is extraneous. Hence Dickie has latterly spoken of a 'set of the aspects of the object' as having the status of 'work of art' conferred upon it.

Part of the plausibility of this theory is precisely that it makes no attempt to offer any restrictive definition of art; it is not the sort of definition which can fall foul of the fringe art described earlier. The music of Cage, the art of Duchamps and Tinguely count as music and art because of the way they are accepted by the art world. The onus of deciding whether or not an artefact is a work of art becomes the responsibility of the art world and not the philosopher. By this analysis of 'work of art' the phil- osopher divests himself of one of the most intractable problems in aesthetics, the problem of the criteria and conditions for art.

But, inevitably, problems remain. One of the more serious objections is that the account is circular. A work of art is defined by reference to the art world. But how do we count a person a member of the art world save through his interest in and concern for works of art? It is by virtue of a serious interest in these artefacts that a person qualifies as a member of the art world. So we require an independent characterisation of the art world in order to get this account off the ground, a characterisa- tion which is, specifically, one which makes no reference to works of art. It is hard to see how this can be done. As it stands the theory is question begging.

It might be argued in extenuation that with an area of human activity as important and as pervasive as the aesthetic, we cannot expect an analysis which is couched in quite other terms. It is very difficult to see how such an analysis could be given without reducing the aesthetic to the non-aesthetic. Consider the parallel difficulties of analysing moral judgements into non-moral terms. Both the aesthetic and the moral are what we might call basic categories of human experience; they are irreducible.

We can take this point without concluding that the art world analysis is thereby vindicated. As I argued in the previous chapter, art and the aesthetic overlap. On any plausible definition of aesthetic experience much which counts as aesthetic experience may not be experience of art. Consequently it may still be possible to give an analysis which embraces both the aesthetic and non- aesthetic liaisons of the concept without circularity. In the chapter on interpretation in the arts I shall defend one of a family of such approaches.

There is a further objection which is independent of the charge of circularity. This second objection depends on attacking the premiss that a distinction between an evaluative and a descriptive sense can be made prior to deciding what a work of art is (in the descriptive sense). When a work of art is presented to the public it is presented as the latest work in a tradition. Thus if John Cage's 'Four minutes 33 seconds' is a piano piece then it continues a tradition which runs back through Bartók and Prokofiev, Chopin, Liszt and Alkan, Schubert and Schumann back to Beethoven and beyond. It is a pretender to a place in that tradition. So if members of the art world present such a work, they imply that it has the sort of quality which the eminent works which compose the tradition display, even if in less high degree. The act of christening, I maintain, is a value-laden activity. Now it may well be that a gallery owner or an editor may merely wish to irritate the public or, in the hope of making money out of a *succès de scandale*, offer his public a work which he knows has no merit whatsoever. But this does not remove the fact that in presenting an artefact as a work of art, he commits himself to the thesis that it has merits of the same type which repay attention in its eminent forebears. Liars also make statements we take to be true and defrauders can make promises. Godparents at christenings make promises they do not intend to keep. But they are still promises.

So if the act of christening a work and thereby enrolling it in the class which is the extension of the descriptive sense of 'work of art' is thought to be itself a value-free activity, as the analysis appears to imply, then the analysis is wrong. Christening implies a valuation. It may even be that there is no neutral way of approaching a work of art prior to deciding upon its merits and that grading is built in to the very act of contemplating a work of art. Contemplation of any sort is a critical activity in that it engages the person in judging the characteristics and features of the object, and in that judgement appraising it. I shall describe this aspect of aesthetic experience in more detail in the next section where I discuss aesthetic attention.

Suppose Robinson Crusoe painted a picture. According to this analysis it could not count as a work of art unless either Crusoe himself belonged to the art world, or the painting was discovered by other explorers who either numbered a member of the art world amongst themselves, or who took it back to civilisation. In all other cases, the work is only potentially a work of art. Equally, the art of the Altamira caves was not art at the time it was produced, but only once it became acknowledged as such by an art world. This point ought not be be confused with the obvious and trivial truth that since nobody alive had the concept of art as we understand it, those remote peoples who painted the Altamira murals, probably in the belief that their hunting would be magically aided, could not recognise what they produced as art. These works became art only when they were found a century ago. This may or may not be counter-intuitive; it makes our assessment of the art of the past counter-factual in style; but certainly it is an implication which needs to be recognised.

Much contemporary art is perhaps best viewed as anti-art. Cage's famous 'piano piece' is more a rude gesture at art than an attempt to continue and develop a tradition; the same can be said for the art of Tinguely and Duchamps, Warhol and, to a lesser extent, Cardew and other extreme figures. Cornelius Cardew objects in particular to the bourgeois associations which art carries. The problem is that these manifestations of art cannot be understood in the same way as much previous art; they belong to a genre more akin to metacriticism or to criticism of the relation of art to society than to art proper. The creators of this type of art would certainly resent their works being given an imprimatur by the art establishment. The status they want is precisely that ambiguous status for which the art world theory finds no place, for according to the art world theory artefacts are either works of art or not, depending entirely on whether they are christened as such by an agent of the art world. Furthermore, the concept can find no application in the case of new genres of art. As we have seen, at various times during the history of art new forms of art have become recognised; most recently the film has been generally recognised as a distinct genre. But how could this be explained on the art world theory? Unquestionably there can be no sub-group within the art world concerned with film whilst that art was in its infancy; only as an art grows to its first maturity, does there grow the habit of commenting on and criticising it until the whole business becomes formalised through the appointment of critics and the publication of journals of criticism. As the art develops so does the corresponding part of the art world until the genre is generally recognised as an independent art form.

The art world theory offers an account of how a work in an existing genre can be given the status of art. It does not give us any explanation of how new forms of art become accepted as types of art. For here the dawning recognition of a new species of art comes simultaneously with the development of the appropriate sub section of the art world. How, then, do new forms of art receive recognition?

AESTHETIC ATTENTION

One answer to this question would be that we regard certain artefacts as works of art because we expect them to repay the sort of attention we lavish on paradigm works of art. We can count the music of Peter Maxwell Davies as music because we think that it will repay the sort of consideration we are accustomed to give to the music of Bach, Beethoven and Brahms. More broadly we recognise the film as a form of art because we see that the best films reward the close attention which we give to works from other branches of the arts.

But what is this special sort of attention which we have labelled aesthetic attention and how does it relate to our response to art? An answer to this might be, simultaneously, an oblique answer to the main question which has preoccupied us, what is a work of art? For if we can pick out a special sort of attention that is appropriate to aesthetic objects then we may define art as those objects

either designed for aesthetic attention or selected by
people with that in mind.

Since the eighteenth century many writers have
thought of disinterestedness as being a defining feature
of aesthetic attention. To look at an object in an aesthetic
sort of way is to ignore any purpose that object might
serve. We cannot, whilst contemplating its aesthetic features, concern ourselves with its suitability to fulfil any
particular function. If I weigh up a book on the grounds
that it has or has not the requisite thickness to prop up a
table leg then I do not have its aesthetic features in the
forefront of my mind. If I appraise a new recording of
Schubert's great C major symphony on the basis of
whether or not it is loud enough to drown the noise the
neighbours are making then I am obviously not concerned with its aesthetic merits.

The historical importance of the idea of disinterestedness is very great. In an influential series of papers,
Jerome Stolnitz[3] argued that two very significant aspects
of modern aesthetics derive from it; the first is the idea of
art as unique and autonomous, and the second is the
broadening of the concept of the aesthetic so as to
include other objects and activities as well as works of art.
For Shaftesbury, who introduced the topic to aesthetics,
the concept was associated with the abandonment of
self-concern which marks the moral agent. We shall, later
in the book, consider the uniqueness of works of art and
the idea that works of art are autonomous. The latter
assumption is perhaps best exemplified in the idea of
practical criticism in which works of art are examined in a
situation where a minimum of external information is
available. For the present, we shall concentrate on what
is still an important consideration in the analysis of aesthetic attention, disinterestedness.

Now it is frequently the case that people choose books
or records or paintings to enjoy. This might seem in-
nocuous but it argues a self-indulgent attitude towards
the arts. Certainly it suggests that the reader approaches
the book with a certain end in view; he reads the book
because it will give him pleasure. For him the book serves

a particular function. This should not be confused with a superficially similar but importantly distinct case, the case where pleasure is the natural and appropriate response to that particular work. Pleasure is the natural and appropriate response to a piece of entertainment music such as a wind serenade or divertimento by Mozart even when it may have concealed depths. So to attend to the work with pleasure in view is only right and proper. But *Othello* or *Measure for Measure* are works of a different category. The comment 'A thoroughly enjoyable evening in the theatre' would imply a failure to understand the play, and a failure to respond to it in the right sort of way. A proper response to either of these plays must be more complex. To use them as the occasion for pleasure would require a fairly blinkered vision of the work and suggests an 'interested' approach. Sometimes, then, this may pre-empt a disinterested concern for the work of art and sometimes not. As we have seen, to feel like certain 'mood' music, as it is called, and to select a record for that purpose is to use the music to perform a certain function. It is, however, not necessarily incompatible with an aesthetic appreciation of the music as long as the response is simultaneously the appropriate response to that particular piece of music. So to attend to a work with a particular interest is not necessarily to exclude the possibility of aesthetic attention.

Consider, however, reading a novel in order to improve one's understanding of man and his relation to his society; to advocate reading novels for this purpose sounds impossibly sententious (in a word, Leavisite) but philosophers are sometimes said to read novels for this reason. If the correlative response to this approach does involve an enriching of one's understanding then such an approach is neither strictly disinterested nor lacking a properly aesthetic element.

There are many other cases where art may be studied for ulterior motives without the aesthetic aspect being thereby excluded. Students prepare for an examination or for an essay by reading a text; far from excluding aesthetic considerations it is precisely aesthetic considerations which are relevant to the preparation. One would have to be quite unreasonably cynical to deny that students of literature sometimes respond aesthetically to the texts they study. Cousins to this sort of activity are reading novels for review, reading them in order to revise them, or reading a novel or a poem and viewing a painting or reading a score in order to decide whether or not it should be put before the public. In all these cases, the activity is commenced with a purpose in mind, but the particular purpose depends upon the aesthetic response of the person in question. Novels and poems will not be published, paintings hung or music performed unless there is a positive aesthetic response from the person who does the vetting.

However in all these cases, the advocate of disinterestedness might argue quite plausibly that all these other purposes we have mentioned are conditional upon the critic first having a disinterested attitude to the work, and that that attitude is, as far as aesthetic response is concerned, quite basic; we must primarily regard the work for its own sake and not as a means to an end. So providing that the defender of disinterestedness does not hold that that attitude cannot co-exist with other 'interested' attitudes, I am inclined to think that part of our approach to art has been caught in this analysis.

One feature which characterises our responses to aesthetic objects is that the response matures. There is a fairly predictable sequence through which a person's taste develops and this does seem to be a general feature of aesthetic experience. A child may begin by reading Beatrix Potter, progress to Defoe, Captain Marryat or to Biggles books, and then graduate to *Jane Eyre* or to *David Copperfield*. But we would be surprised at the precocity of a child who admired Jane Austin, George Eliot or Tolstoy. These usually await a maturer taste. In music Mozart may appear at both ends. What seems 'pretty' to the tyro seems unbearably poignant to the experienced listener. However the detail of this pilgrim's progress may vary, it is uncommon for the process to be reversed. Who comes to prefer *Coral Island* to *Anna*

Karenina, or the Tchaikovski ballets to late Beethoven?

Critics of this thesis may point to the fact that we often retain an enthusiasm for music, literature or films which we know are not of the very best. I may continue to delight in the *Nutcracker Ballet* (the complete version, of course) whilst admitting that late Beethoven gives me a more profound experience. Here we touch on the striking and mysterious way in which certain works of art 'speak' to us and become, in a manner of talking, part of an identity. It is this that makes the ending of Fahrenheit 451 so poignant, for the point is not just that *David Copperfield* can survive through being memorised. By adopting the name of the novel he has learnt, the memoriser symbolically represents the fact that the books we know and love form part of our identity. So there is art which I admire and art which I love. There is also a third category, namely that art which is especially significant because of the associations it has. Now it is only the first category that customarily exhibits the progression of taste: and in presenting this thesis we set aside and perhaps implicitly devalue those responses to art which depend upon personal idiosyncrasies. (Perhaps I should make clear that, of course, there is much art which we both love and admire.)

Even granted the restricted validity of this thesis, as it stands it casts no light on our central problem, the problem of rendering intelligible the concept of the aesthetic attitude. For, as I made clear when we began to discuss the question of maturation, it is primarily a thesis about our response to art and not about our attitude to the aesthetic: furthermore, it is not a thesis about our response to an individual work of art so much as about our response to or experience of a whole class of works of art. One reason for thinking it may be especially relevant to the more distant goal of achieving an understanding of what it is for an artefact to be a work of art is that maturation does not seem to be a characteristic of our appreciation of aesthetic objects which are not works of art, such as landscaped. Here taste reigns supreme uncomplicated by various orderings in our evaluation of the various objects.

Aesthetic experience and response are not of the first importance in our immediate inquiry. The attitude we adopt to a work is largely within our control and we can approach both good and bad works with the appropriate Gestalt for an aesthetic object: but our response depends very largely upon factors such as the quality of the object and our receptivity at the time we encounter it, factors which we cannot control in the same way. So to use a characteristic which enters into our response to aesthetic objects in the definition of a work of art is to risk a definition of, at most, 'successful work of art', and this is not what we want. It is therefore important to try to transform the maturation principle into a form where it characterises the attitude to art rather than the response or experience. The way to do this is, I suggest, to make it part and parcel of the approach to a work of art that we endeavour to place that work within a series of works running from the accessible to the profound. Our initial encounter places the work within a tradition of works in that genre, within this tradition each work both depends upon past achievements and, in a way, surmounts them. I have touched on this before and shall expand on the theme again when I come to discuss the criticism of art. A further feature is that in initially placing the work as difficult or as immediately rewarding we form expectations about what it offers and what our response will be, a judgement which we may later find cause to revise.

Maturation thus implies a serial ordering of art. The aesthetic attitude to art absorbs this fact by presuming that the work about to be examined will be given a place in the series. Sometimes the reader or listener will realise that the work extends his experience of the art beyond the point for which he is currently prepared. More often it will be more easily understood and placed within a familiar section of the order. The music of Elliott Carter and the music of Zelenka will be approached with different expectations. The first composes notoriously difficult and complex contemporary works, the latter composed idiosyncratic music of the late Baroque which, though surprising, requires no new developments in the taste of the average informed listener.

In the first chapter of the *Biographia Literaria*, Coleridge acknowledges his debt to his old headmaster at Christ's Hospital:

I learnt from him that Poetry, even that of the loftiest and, seemingly, that of the wildest odes, had a logic of its own, as severe as that of science; and more difficult, because more subtle, more complex, and dependent on more and more fugitive causes. In the truly great poets, he would say, there is a reason assignable, not only for every word, but for the position of every word;

In this passage Coleridge epitomises that fundamental property of works of art which, following Bradley, I shall call 'density'. The assumption is that all parts of a work of art are relevant for in all we see the creator's hand. This presupposes that we have, at least a rough intuitive conception of what the boundaries of any particular works of art are. The prop-men who walk on and off the stage in a Chinese theatre are not part of the play any more than is the proscenium arch in a western theatre, or the beams of light in a darkened cinema. Nor are the conductor's taps on his baton on the rostrum the first notes of the symphony. Conventions settle what counts as the work and what does not. But within the work, each part has its place; each note, each word, each brush stroke has its own function in the whole.

Certainly the skill of the critic lies *inter alia* in his ability to tease out the significance of the detail; it is exhibited in this quotation from Middleton Murray's essay on *Anthony and Cleopatra*.[4] Of the lines,

Now boast thee, death, in thy possession lies
A lass unparalleled.

he writes:

Every other great poet the world has known, I dare swear, would have written, would have been compelled to write: 'A queen unparallel'd.' But Shakespeare's daimon compels him otherwise: compels him not consciously to remember, but instinctively to body forth in utterance, the Cleopatra who dreams, and is a girl.

What we have called 'density' is evidently closely related to another feature that works of art possess, namely 'unity'. The two requirements are not identical. There might be a reason for the choice of any particular word or for its particular position in a line without the resultant poem being conspicuous for its unity. But generally one important reason for the placing of an image, a brush-stroke or a particular melodic motif is that it enhances the overall unity of the work.

Unity is, of course, a very important element in the criticism of the arts and the particular form it takes will vary from art to art. Amongst musicians and musicolo- gists, for instance, there has been a lengthy discussion of the extent to which musical unity depends upon the transformation and development of basic thematic material. Partly through the compositional methods of Schoenberg and the Second Viennese school, critics have come to admire and seek for thematic interconnec- tions between the various parts of a movement or a work. In a very highly organised work such as a late Haydn symphony or quartet or one of Beethoven's mature works, very little of the melodic material will be unrelated to the basic themes. A basic tune may be inverted, played backwards, shortened or lengthened. Parallels can be found in the other arts. A critic will show how the same ideas and preoccupations keep recurring over and over again in a Shakespeare play so that each section can be shown to be a reflection on and a development of the basic themes. What we can say in general is that, as a consequence of this interrelatedness, cuts and altera- tions become progressively more risky the higher the quality of the work. The more unified a work, the more such changes will have deleterious effects, *ceteris paribus;* conversely, to the extent that such alterations improve or do not damage, the work is not so highly unified as it might be. We need to make the provision about all things being equal simply to set aside cases where a work can be improved by replacing a section which is rather pedestrian in its material by a section which shows inspiration. Michael Tippett sent his libretto for the oratorio 'A Child of our Time' to T.S. Eliot for comment. Eliot declined to make alterations since the quality of his writing would stick out like a sore thumb. Now it is quite conceivable that Tippett's libretto is unified whilst still being the case that Eliot's interpolations would improve it by introducing verse of a genuine quality, though at the cost of unity. However this is a price we will sometimes willingly pay. For Tippett's purposes, of course, it is important that the verse does not distract from the music and uneven verse might well do that.

The assumption of unity is an ideal requirement in a work; few works are of such quality that no replacements or alterations are possible which will improve the work. It is precisely the ideal nature of the requirement which makes it such a plausible candidate for a factor in the aesthetic attitude; we approach works with the ideal of unity in mind and scold them for failing it. But having a weather eye open for the sort of significance exemplified in those lines of Shakespeare quoted above is integral to the aesthetic attitude.

However this argument needs both qualification and expansion. Certain large-scale works, though members of the set of paradigms which we have in mind when we discuss art, nevertheless are flawed. There are one or two feeble numbers in any of the great Mozart operas; *Hamlet* contains some of Shakespeare's less mature verse; many think *War and Peace* is flawed by the self-conscious theorising about history which punctuates it. Indeed it is hard to find a large-scale work which could not be improved by certain alterations replacing some existing material by new material in the master's best vein. A very familiar controversy in music revolves around the last movement of Beethoven's *Ninth*

Symphony. But our attitude to cuts and improvements is ambivalent. To an extent we have grown fond of the works as they stand, warts and all, and our affection for them is bound up with their familiarity. Equally we may well feel that 'le style est l'homme même' and that no alterations by another hand could possibly be satisfactory. Even so the consensus, at least in music, has moved towards a deeper awareness of the manifold and subtle ways in which a great work of art is unified.

One final point is that the intensity of a work may properly vary with the intensity of its unity. A work cannot consist of one single constant climax; the highlights require background and it is in the background that, in theory, changes ought to be possible without so much affecting the work. Change the great soliloquies in *Macbeth* and you change the character of the work. Perhaps nobody except a theatre director would consider making changes in the porter's scene, but if alterations and cuts are to be made without too deleterious consequences it is there that they can be made. (I hope I am not overestimating present-day's directors' respect for the text.)

The correlative of the attitude which seeks density in a work and castigates it where it falls short is an aesthetic experience of the work where there is an interaction between the reader, viewer or listener's experience of the detail and his experience of the whole. We may follow C. L. Stevenson here and contrast synoptic and dissective attention. If I listen carefully to one part in a quartet, say the viola part, with the others relegated to a haze of sonority, then Stevenson speaks of my listening with dissective attention. If I concentrate on the metre or internal rhyme or alliteration of a poem, then in all three of these tasks I am reading dissectively. If I attempt to read the line taking these into account whilst keeping myself aware of the other elements in the poem, then I read it with synoptic attention and my overall experience, my 'net impression' of the work, may be richer for the dissective attention which preceded it. In this, Stevenson has identified a crucially important factor in our experience of art and one

which has considerable implications for a study of aesthetic attitude. For taking an aesthetic attitude demands
that I contemplate a work of art with these forms of
attention at the ready. The assumption of density within a
work carries the implication that the work will repay an
exercise of dissective and synoptic attention in turn.

Both unity and density are properties of works of art; it
is works of art which we expect to be created in such a
way that the detail is crucial to its overall effect; works of
art thus display a unity which we do not expect from
natural objects whose arrangement is fortuitous. A lakeland view, for example, may have great beauty but we do
not expect that the placing of a single tree necessarily
contributes to the beauty of the whole in quite the same
way as a single image in a poem contributes to its total
effect. Now in a sense, of course, what we see is made up
of detail; in that sense it is the detail that determines the
whole just as any whole is made of its parts. But the thesis
thus trivialised is the thesis mis-stated. Works of art benefit from the unconscious processes of their creator, processes which confer upon them a unity and a structure
beyond what the creator could control. It is a fact about a
great poem, picture or piece of music that it is unified in
many ways, and there is ample evidence that a critic may
spot coherences of which the creator was unaware.
Schoenberg[5] was sufficiently worried by an apparent lack
of relation between the two main themes of the *First
Chamber Symphony* to contemplate rewriting:

About twenty years later I saw the true relationship. It is of such
a complicated nature that I doubt whether any composer
would have cared deliberately to construct a theme in this
way; but our subconscious does it involuntarily.

In Freud's words, art 'is dipped in the unconscious'.

We cannot expect similar 'deep' connections within a
landscape. If one particular line is mirrored in a corresponding contour on an opposite hill then this is fortuitous. Unity is a feature of art of quality and its place in the
aesthetic attitude pertains only to the aesthetic attitude
we adopt towards art and not towards 'nature'.

The requirement that the aesthetic attitude must be disinterested requires some abstraction from ordinary considerations of utility and purpose; the final candidate we shall consider as a necessary condition of adopting the aesthetic attitude requires a similar bracketing off of normal human concerns and reactions. This is the idea of 'distancing'. The protagonist of 'psychical distancing', Bullough, used the example of being in a fog at sea. One can abstract those aspects of the situation which are aesthetically appealing; we can admire the shapes and the tonality in the swirling fog whilst setting aside the physical danger of a collision followed by the sinking of the ship. Certainly something akin to psychical distancing is familiar when we are attending to ordinary objects, vistas or situations and become suddenly aware of their aesthetic aspects. To be in a crowded room and to become suddenly aware of its possibilities as a film set or to see the chiaroscuro in a city street at night with the inter-play of light and dark, of mist, fog or smoke can be a powerful aesthetic experience (and one which is dispelled by modern street lighting). But frequently this type of experience is itself mediated by works of art. Whistler and Turner made us aware of the aesthetic features of fog and mist, and Hitchcock of the exciting and unnerving qualities of dimly-lit streets. As far as works of art are concerned it is primarily in the theatre that any case can be made for distancing as a part of the aesthetic attitude. The usual example given is that of a spectator at *Othello* drawn to intervene to save Desdemona but through distancing, separating himself sufficiently from the action in order not to intervene. Anybody who intervened to the extent of shooting Iago, as reportedly once happened in Baltimore, has ceased to regard the dramatic presentation aesthetically.

Bullough conceived of a balance between over-distancing to the point where the critic becomes too detached an observer of the work, and under-distancing where the critic is too involved. It is hard to see the matter in quite these terms. Certainly the spectator in Baltimore was highly involved in the stage production; in general, if not in this particular case, we might not regard this as a bad thing. We certainly would not say that a man who weeps at a tragedy is responding in an inappropriate way. But then equally a very detached critic might see things in the play which could escape a committed observer, and what he sees be highly relevant to an intelligent judgement. Of both we could say that there are aspects of the work which escape him, but of neither would we wish to say that his reaction is 'unaesthetic'.

Consider a jealous husband on whom the effect of *Othello* is merely to cause him to dwell upon his wife's peccadillos. If he were to reflect more generally on the problems of marital fidelity then we would not be inclined to dismiss his reaction as irrelevant to the aesthetic considerations. By distancing himself he may be able to reflect more calmly on these features of the play. Now there is a reason why we do not object if the considerations are general and it is because then the husband approaches the common background and motivation which the playwright can depend upon when he writes. If indeed insane jealousy were common and could be expected in the *homme moyen sensual* in the audience then it would no longer be an irrelevance; the writer will be expected to have written with these common human attitudes in mind.

This 'blocking out' of ordinary practical considerations is conceived as a voluntary act on the part of the spectator by the protagonists of 'psychical distancing'. But as George Dickie points out, there is no reason to suppose that this involves a special faculty brought into play only when we have aesthetic concerns. It is simply a matter of either paying attention to the work or not paying attention to the work. Letting one's mind wander on to practical considerations such as marital difficulties simply is not paying attention.

So far, the onus is placed upon the spectator, he must distance himself from the events on the stage. But it is questionable as to whether this is within his gift. A convincing drama could perhaps sweep you off your feet, making you forget momentarily that you are in the theatre. We might particularly admire a play that can create that sort of illusion: whether this is frequent or infrequent or, whether, indeed it occurs at all is a question which is both relevant to this particular issue and to the more general issues of artistic representation.

If the phenomenon of aesthetic distancing occurs at all during the adoption of an aesthetic attitude to a work of art it occurs in a small proportion of cases. It is implausible to think that it could ever be appropriate in reading poetry or in listening to music. The only cases where it seems remotely likely are in the film and theatre. Elsewhere it is perhaps at most part of the preparation one might make for concentrating on the aesthetic qualities of the surroundings but it certainly cannot be a general feature of having an aesthetic attitude to an object.

REPRESENTATION

In the course of discussing one putative characterisation of the aesthetic attitude I have introduced some problems about representation and illusion in drama. Now is the time to examine these questions more closely and the debate as to what constitutes a work of art thus moves to a new area. From now on we shall be concerned with representational theories of art. The word 'representation' is sometimes used to translate the Greek word 'mimesis'; 'imitation' is also sometimes used though neither translation is entirely happy.

The representational arts are primarily literature and the visual arts. Literature includes not only poetry and the novel but also drama. In the visual arts we include not only painting and sculpture but also the film. Consequently the representational arts cut across the classification we offered in chapter two: some performing arts fall within the representational arts, some do not: to some the type token distinction applies and to some it does not. Some thinkers have tried to enlarge the scope of the representational arts by absorbing within them arts such as music by proposing that the representational element in music lies in its ability to imitate or represent the emotions. But we must postpone a discussion of this important question until we begin our examination of Expressionism.

In the sections that follow I propose to discuss a group of issues relating to the various representational arts. The problems debated have this in common, they all arise from the representational nature of the art in question. Through analysing these questions we may draw conclusions about the nature of a convincing representation, about the way art affects us, about the lessons we learn from art, and finally about the strengths and weaknesses of representationalist theories in general.

Illusion, pretence and dramatic representation[6]
I have spoken as though illusion is a possibility in the theatre, as though the audience might really believe that it was watching events actually taking place. The parallel situation for a televised dramatic performance or for a filmed performance is easy to conceive. Now in the previous section I considered the argument that such an illusion was inimical to the proper adoption of the aesthetic attitude to the presentation. We might further consider whether such an illusion ever occurs and whether, if it does, we should count it as a success on the part of writer, actors or directors. If not, then we must ask ourselves what we mean when we say that a play is 'convincing'.

Dr Johnson's robust reply is well known. 'The truth is that the spectators are always in their senses, and know, from the first act to the last, that the stage is only a stage and that the players are only players.' If this were so then there would be no problem. No yokel would try to intervene, but neither would there be the familiar tightening of the throat as the hero is in danger, the relief as he escapes, and the tears at a victim's fate. How do we understand these strange symptoms?

In *Problems of the Self* Bernard Williams says 'What Sir Laurence does to Miss Smith is [something like] pretending to strangle her; but Othello does not pretend to strangle Desdemona, and it would be a very different play if he did'. 'Something like' is disarming here, of course, but it does suggest that Williams thinks that light can be cast on the concept of dramatic representation by introducing the concept of pretence. Sometimes at least pretence successfully deceives another person; I might pretend to be wealthier than I am and succeed in misleading my creditors; frauds depend upon their ability to pretend successfully. But it is clear, I think, that successful deceptive pretence stands to dramatic representation rather as *trompe l'oeil* effects stand to representation in the visual arts. Both are exceptional. A particular style of painting can give the spectator the illusion that what he is looking at is a real bank note or a real door. Successful *trompe l'oeil* effects are rare; the painter usually needs to paint a shallow object like a letter rack or a dollar bill for otherwise movement round the object rapidly discloses that is is actually flat.

Sometimes pretending is attempting to deceive, sometimes not. If I pretend to be a bear to amuse a small child then I do not intend to deceive him into thinking I am a real bear; my purpose is to amuse him by mildly frightening him, but it is my wild behaviour and the pleasure of a game of pretence which jointly achieve this effect. This form of pretending verges on dramatic representation. If I say to somebody 'Pretend to be angry' I am inviting him to act as though he were angry. I am unlikely to be taken in by the performance since I have invited it. If, however, he is a really superb actor then we could imagine saying, 'My goodness, I really thought you were angry'. Two important points have emerged. First, there is a form of pretence that is very close to dramatic representation but lacks the institutional hallmarks of drama such as stage-setting. In this form of pretence, deception is not a motive. Sometimes the audience forgets for a moment or for a longer period that it is a dramatic representation that they are watching. Perhaps, and this is the second point, we should be speaking of illusion rather than deception in this context.

Brecht regarded theatrical illusion as a menace to be controlled by the stressing of conventions; back projection, songs, choreography, etc. enable the writer to ensure that the audience never forgets that it is merely a play that it is watching, and thereby to reflect on its various morals. Illusion is not an effect that the writer is necessarily attempting to achieve, and indeed the circumstances of the theatre are such that he could hardly depend upon achieving it. For one reason, many plays are familiar to the audience and they know the action, they therefore can predict the speeches and the action of the protagonists; if there is to be a surprise it will come in the way in which the actor or director chooses to vary or add to the performing traditions. Now all this is inimical to our seeing the actor as engaged in pretence. It would be odd indeed if a pretender's words and actions were predictable to that degree. For deceptive pretence to be at all successful, then, the pretender's behaviour has to be such as could without oddity be expected from an ordinary person who is not pretending. Now one crucial feature about human behaviour is the relative unpredictability of speech compared with that which exists where an actor speaks from a text. If acting is like deceptive pretending then the similarity must be between peripheral forms of acting, such as extemporisation, and peripheral forms of pretence which tend to collapse into conscious role playing – dramatic representation; these are cases of pretence where no deceit is intended and any illusion is accidental.

Only where an illusion is intended can we speak of the actor pretending in the central sense of that word, for it is then that the actor intends to deceive. But such circumstances, as I have argued, must be infrequent, if they exist at all.

A final consideration which makes the theory that dramatic representation is a form of pretence untenable is connected with the way in which we gauge success. A successful pretence is one which is liable to deceive. I might indeed pretend to be somebody or to do something where the possibility of deception is so remote as to be ruled out. I may pretend to be a three-toed sloth, a gnat or a bear but I am most unlikely to deceive the smallest child into thinking that I really am a three-toed sloth, gnat or bear. But here we grade pretence as good, bad or indifferent. Marcel Marceau is superb at pretending to be a man walking against a wind, but he is neither successful nor unsuccessful. But we can talk about an actor's successful assumption of a part. If dramatic representation is simply deceptive pretence then this must mean that his behaviour would deceive the average onlooker who is not guarding against deception.

But in fact it is the critic who is aware that Olivier is acting, and can see how he has changed and added to traditional ideas about the role, who can see the skill and intelligence in each movement and intonation, who is best fitted to judge the success of the performance and not the tyro who is utterly taken in. That is, to the extent that the performance deceives us we are unable to measure the success of the performance, its internal consistency and so on. Characteristically, a great actor surprises us by behaviour which only subsequently we realise to be integrated at a deeper level with the sort of character he conceives the dramatic persona to be. In the film *Tunes of Glory* Alec Guinness plays the role of an extrovert, feckless, hail-fellow-well-met acting C-in-C, who is replaced by a more sensitive and over-anxious officer as C-in-C of a Highland Regiment. Eventually his successor commits suicide because he cannot obtain the loyalty of the men. Guinness, realising his own part in the tragedy, is led away by two other officers with his face covered by his hands. Overt expression of grief would be out of character; but Guinness' interpretation, at first surprising, strikes one suddenly as a dramatic *tour de force*. But it is because we are not deceived into thinking that we are spectators of actual events that we can see what it is that is so crucial to the aesthetic appreciation of the scene, namely, the skill and insight of the actor. It is the skill of the performance that we admire, and deception is the enemy of this recognition.

In pretending, a person often pretends to have a particular characteristic at a particular time, he pretends to be angry when he is not; he may pretend to be doing something when he is not; he may pretend to be marking essays when he is really reading a newspaper. It is of the essence of this sort of pretence that the pretender adopts certain behaviour which he thinks is appropriate to the abilities, emotions, activities and responses of the state – àctivity in which he is pretending to be or do. But the actor is, as I have said, in a counter-identical situation. It is not Sir Laurence pretending to be jealous, but Sir Laurence 'pretending' to be Othello being jealous. The actor is 'pretending' to be another individual in that state or performing that activity; the concept of dramatic representation is thus probably more closely related to impersonation than to pretence. The importance of this is that the counter-identical situation is one in which we can properly raise the aesthetic questions of consistency and unity amongst the various parts of the actor's performance. We can ask whether Othello as interpreted at this stage of his career could reasonably be a person who does what Othello does at the end of the play and so on. But we do not raise the question of whether the pretender's behaviour is consistent with his behaviour later or earlier unless we are interested in uncovering his deceit. And deceit is not an aesthetically relevant issue.

It may be tempting to equate success in dramatic performance with internal consistency in the interpretation of the role. This is an obvious conclusion and was my own first thought about the matter. But presumably there can be consistent but shallow performances and these we would want to discount. It is the surprising consistency which we so often admire as my illustration from the work of Alec Guinness was intended to show.

Finally there are certain analogies between dramatic representation and representation in the fine arts. A picture may represent what philosophers call 'an intentional object'. This is a term of art. Thus a picture may represent a fictional or mythological object and the object of the painting may then be said to have but an intentional existence; consequently the intentional nature of the object of a picture is such that from the fact that a painting represents x it does not follow that x exists. Equally it does not follow from the fact that an actor represents x that x has or still does exist. There are stage representations of both *Richard III* and *Pyramus and Thisbe*. Now if the audience were to judge the success of the actor's assumption of a role on his ability to deceive them then really successful acting would be judged only in retrospect. Not until the final curtain nudged the audience back into reality would they recall that it was a play they had seen and only then will they begin to assess the performance. Ideally they might like to compare the playing with the original; that would only be possible where the original not only actually existed but could be inspected. Since this is normally impossible, the only criterion of success can be the achievement of illusion.

My argument has been that whilst a successful perfor-mance may well occasionally produce the illusion in the audience that it is watching real events, its members normally oscillate between a temporary and unreflective illusion and a consideration of the art and artifice of the actor. It may well be, though I have not argued that here, that an intelligent reaction to a play involves a dialectic movement between illusion and reflection. But I certainly do not want to endorse the notion of suspension of dis-belief; the illusion is not foisted on himself by a member of the audience; he does not choose it; it is short lived and unintended. Finally the great performance, like the great performance in any of the performing arts, sums up and modifies a tradition of interpretations. This will pass the critic by if he is in the grip of an illusion.

I have said little about the very difficult question as to how the play-goer becomes involved in the play. A simi-lar question arises with respect to the film-goer or the reader of fiction or biography. One obviously important feature is the way we identify with a character or a group of characters so that his, her or their fate matters to us. We begin to see the action through the eyes of the hero and fear and hate the villain. This is not an inevitable feature of art, of course, but it is important when the narrative interest is crucial. It is certainly the case that if we cease to be absorbed in the narrative, we often no longer follow the fate of characters with such enthusiasm. Whilst successful performance may well occasionally produce the illusion in members of the audience that they are watching real events, the audience normally oscillates between a temporary and unreflective illusion and a conscious consideration of the art and artifice of the action. In a quotation from Fontanelle, Hume neatly summarises the contrasting attitudes we may take and incidentally stresses the role of identification or 'attachment', as he calls it:'We weep for the misfortune of a hero to whom we are attached. In the same instant we comfort ourselves by reflecting that it is nothing but a fiction.

Pictorial representation
As we have seen, pictorial representation is intentional in character. Painters have painted Greek gods and godesses who are no longer widely thought to exist. But the fact that the object of a painting does not exist does not, of course, prevent the painting being a painting of that object. This elementary observation is central to one important and interesting philosophical puzzle: What makes a picture a representation of whatever it is a representation of? What makes Goya's portrait of Wellington a portrait of Wellington, and not of some other worthy? Is it that it resembles Wellington? Is it in some way related to the fact that Wellington sat for it? Or is it simply that Goya entitled it a portrait of Wellington? In these answers lie encapsulated the three theories I shall consider and which I entitle respectively, the Resemblance, the Causal and the Intentionalist theories.

Resemblance
Is Goya's picture of Wellington a picture of Wellington because it resembles Wellington? More generally, is x a representation of y if and only if x resembles y? There are some fairly conclusive objections to this suggestion. (i) Everything resembles everything else in some way. After all any two objects resemble each other at least in being extended in space. So we need at least to specify more closely what the degree and form of resemblance must

be, for we would hardly count x to be a representation of y simply because both are extended in space. Should we then say that x is a representation of y if and only if x and y resemble each more than either resembles anything else? Clearly this would be false. A picture resembles another picture more than it resembles the sitter whom it represents. For one thing both pictures are effectively two dimensional, both are composed of pigment upon canvas, both are framed and in neither can the reverse of the sitter be seen, and so on. So the nature of the resemblance needs to be filled out; x represents y if and only if x resembles y in respects . . . What are these respects? First, there need be no correspondence in size. Many portraits are less than life-size, and presumably there has never been a life-size landscape. Then again a picture may be in monochrome so that the colours in the picture need not match the colours of the presented object. Even when the appearance of the pigments seems to match the colours of the represented object, the artist may have had to allow for the fact that colours in close proximity change their tonality in a way which may not be the case when larger areas of colour are adjacent to one another. The artist's representation is dictated by the medium he chooses. An oil sketch will require that the distinction between figures and background be made in a different way than it would if the picture was in monochrome. The representation depends upon the relations between figure and figure or figure and ground in a given medium.

A third way of filling out the resemblance theory might be to say that x represents y if the relative position of the features in the picture corresponds to the relative positions of the features of the object being depicted. Thus the two eyes of the sitter have the same relative distance from the brow, nose, mouth, etc. in the picture as in reality. However this expansion of the condition falls foul of caricature. Cartoons and caricatures deliberately distort the observed features of the object, yet they remain representations of that object.

Perhaps a picture is a representation of an object if and only if somebody who knows y would identify x as a representation of y. Some questions have been begged here; we have used the word representation in both analysans and analysandum and so any formal analysis along these lines is circular. But there are other and more immediate objections to this form of resemblance theory which make a more elaborate and closely argued thesis based on recognition otiose. The condition is simultaneously too restrictive and too liberal. There are representations which nobody would be able to recognise as representations of whatever they represent. For instance, there are children's representations of aunts, uncles, neighbours and so on. If a child draws a stick man and says 'This is Uncle George', then it is a representation of Uncle George even if nobody would recognise the picture as a picture of Uncle George. So the thesis is too restrictive.

Then again the thesis is too liberal. Of a portrait of a former Principal of my College, a colleague remarked that it resembles the former Visitor more than the sitter. So on the resemblance criterion the picture represents an object quite distinct from the object who was the sitter. It allows us to say that a painting represents an object in a way which does not accord with our ordinary application of these concepts. Equally, if one did not know the conventions of caricatures of Churchill it would be easy to misidentify a caricature as a representation of a bulldog (which it more nearly resembles in the relevant (?) ways) than Churchill, whom it actually represents.

One final nail in the coffin of the resemblance theory: if x resembles y, then y resembles x. The relation of resemblance is symmetrical. But the relation of representation is not symmetrical for if x represents y it does not follow that y represents x.

Causality

Those features of a picture, in virtue of which we say it resembles or is a likeness of a particular person, comprise the picture's descriptive content. The genetic character of a picture is determined by the causal chain of events leading to its production. In the case of photographs and portraits we say that the picture is of the person who was photographed or who sat for the portrait. The same relation presumably holds between a perception and the perceived object. This relation between picture and person clearly depends entirely on the genetic character of the picture. Without attempting a definition, we can say that for a picture to be *of* a person, the person must serve significantly in the causal chain leading to the picture's production and also serve as object for the picture. The second clause is to prevent all of an artist's painting from being of the artist. I will shortly say a bit more about how I understand this relation, which I designate with the italicized 'of'. (David Kaplan, 'Quantifying In,' L. Linsky ed., *Reference and Morality*, Oxford U.P. (1971), p.132.

Suppose the artist sits before the model and, eyeing her from time to time, begins to draw. This, I think we would agree, is the most straightforward sort of causal chain we are familiar with, and in most cases this gives a portrait of the sitter. But the result could still be a portrait of somebody else. In *The Prime of Miss Jean Brodie* the besotted art master produces a portrait of Miss Brodie even though the ostensible model is one of his pupils and not Miss Brodie at all. Even the most favourable case for a causal link may not guarantee that the picture is a picture of the object which the artist perceives constantly during his work. It is also a necessary condition of the representation being of the sitter that he is trying to paint the sitter and not somebody else. My example from Muriel Spark's novel in fact meets this condition; the artist tries to paint the model but, moved by unconscious desires, actually paints somebody else. However we deal with this extremely marginal case, the intentions of the artist clearly have a place in the causal narrative in a way which Kaplan does not seem to recognise. However deviously, the artist's intentions play a part in deciding what the picture represents.

Some uneasiness about this is evident in the way in which Kaplan speaks of the sitter serving 'as object for the picture'. Can this idea of 'serving as object' be analysed in terms of the causal chain which he is at pains to emphasise, or is it an additional condition? If it is the latter, as seems likely, how is it to be explained? My guess is that it covertly introduces the intentions of the artist for it is he, surely, who gives the painting its object. A causal theory of representation shares with casual theories of knowledge, belief and memory one overwhelming disadvantage: it provides no explanation of how it is that the picture has a content which 'reflects' what is represented.

We are, I think, entitled to demand from Kaplan a detailed specification of the causal link which holds between object and picture. Is it significant that the artist uses a brush but not that it is a camel hair brush? Is it part of the causal process that he holds the brush at arm's length to get an impression of the relative sizes of the sitter's features? It is presumably part of the relevant causal process that he uses blue and flake white pigments but not that they were made by Windsor & Newton.

Kaplan is an extensionalist here and a picture of a mythical object is not, in his view, a picture of anything at all. But philosophical problems are not to be dodged in this way. We need an explanation of the ordinary sense of 'representation' in which we can say that a picture of Venus is a representation of Venus and is different from a representation of Pallas Athene. This matters to the art historian, the connoisseur, the critic and the ordinary art lover because without such a concept of representation much of the work vital to understanding art cannot begin. Iconography has enriched our knowledge and appreciation of art. This may not matter to Kaplan but it matters to anybody with a serious interest in aesthetics.

Both resemblance and causal theories ultimately founder on the fact that there are pictures whose objects have a merely intentional existence. How can there be either resemblance with or a causal path from an object which is mythological and which has never had any material existence? It is certainly hard to see how a reference to the intentions of the artist can be embedded in a causal sequence without the sequence thereby ceasing to be purely causal. If these criticisms are just, they suggest that we ought to consider an analysis based squarely upon the concept of the artist's intention.

A story about a primary school art class may provide a convenient and amusing entrée.

Teacher: What are you drawing?
Child: God.
Teacher: But nobody knows what God looks like.
Child (Testily): No, of course not. But they will after they've seen my drawing, won't they?

We may feel torn in two directions by this story. On the one hand, if the child attempted to draw God, then God is what the picture represented. The child has spoken, and his intentions determine the answer to the question, what is this a picture of? On the other hand, experts on the Deity seem to agree that He has no physical existence, and hence is not the sort of object that can be represented. Even atheists, who grant Him existence only in an intentionalist sort of way, would agree about the sort of existence He would have if He existed.

Intentionalism
Shall we then say that what makes a picture a representation of x is that the artist intended it as a representation of x?

In many cases, of course, we have no way of establishing the subject of a picture, and the picture of an unknown nobleman or an unidentified landscape remains unknown or unidentified. But note that we presume here that the artist had a specific nobleman or landscape in mind. If the nobleman or landscape were 'imaginary', then the titles 'Picture of a Nobleman' and 'Landscape' would pick out the object represented in a perfectly satisfactory way. The representation is as specific as the artist decrees.

Elsewhere the conventions governing depiction may make it possible to pick out, say, religious subjects. A popular handbook on the iconography of the late sixteenth century, the *Iconologia* of Cesare Ripa, gives a list of the various ways of representing figures. Faith is to be represented by a seated woman with a chalice in her right hand, resting her left hand on a book, and with the world beneath her feet. Clio, the Muse of History, should be represented as a figure with a laurel wreath, trumpet and book. In other cases the painter may give the work a title which enables us to settle the object being represented. However on occasion the artist's title may be overruled. If he painted a picture of Pallas Athene, recognizable as a helmeted figure, and later described the picture as a picture of Diana we are not bound to take his later description; he has most likely forgotten or is perhaps engaged in a bizarre joke. What we would say in these circumstances is that he intended to paint Pallas Athene. What claims he makes are only part of the evidence for his intentions.

Suppose, now, he asks for a postcard of Canterbury because he intends to paint Canterbury cathedral but, unbeknown to him, is sent one of Gloucester instead. The advocate of a causal analysis surely now has the right answer. It is true that the artist intended to paint Canterbury cathedral and yet surely true that, in fact, he has painted Gloucester cathedral. The intentional criterion now gives the wrong answer. However, it is also true of the artist that he intends to paint the cathedral that is pictured on this postcard, and it is because this informs all the actions he makes in painting that we think it right to say that this is the cathedral he has depicted. If asked what cathedral is on the postcard he will reply, wrongly, 'Canterbury'. So he will simultaneously say that he intends to paint this cathedral and that the very same action of painting counts as painting what he intends to paint, namely Canterbury cathedral. His characterisation of the task he is engaged in is faulty. He thinks that his actions carry out his intention when they do not; they are at odds with his prior intention.

But there is a description at the detailed level which gives the right answer. He intends to depict this cathedral which happens to be Gloucester and it will be a representation of Gloucester even if it happens, because he is a poor draughtsman, to look like Canterbury by mistake. The more we break down an action into the sequence of detailed action by which the agent achieves or aims to achieve his end, the closer we get to a description of what he has done which will coincide with a description of what he intended to do. At such a point, intention will not give us the wrong answer.

But the obvious rejoinder is to ask why we should choose the detailed intention-description rather than the broader one. The reason is that we wish to know what has been intentionally achieved. In this respect representation is very like 'thinking of' or 'imagining' in that there cannot be a gap between intention and achievement. I might mistakenly think of Gloucester cathedral when I am invited to think of Canterbury, of course, but at the level 'thinking of a building with such and such characteristics' there cannot be an error; this comes out in the fact that we have no locution like 'representing by accident' any more than we have one for 'thinking of x by accident'. Mistakes are like misnamings in these cases, for at the detailed level if I intend to think of a building with such and such characteristics then I necessarily do unless I am lying or teasing, and the same holds of representation.

It might seem as though, on this account, representation will collapse, as it does for Goodman, into denotation. This is not so. A representation might be intelligible only to the representer, and others have to be told what is being represented. Denotation cannot be private in this way. It is invariably a public act even if the conventions which make this a denotation are newly minted. For denotation occurs in the context of a language, and language is a public matter with pre-existing conventions of reference. None of these conditions holds in the case of representation.

Max Black objects to an analysis of representation in terms of the artist's intentions on the grounds that it is circular. Since what the artist intends is to produce a representation of some specific object, a statement of what he intends cannot be made independently of a description of his intention to produce a representation of this specific object. The notion of representation thus reappears in the analysandum. Were I offering an analysis of representation this would be a just objection. I am not; indeed I am not persuaded that an adequate analysis in quite independent terms is a possibility. Our task is simply that of providing a criterion for deciding what a picture represents, and any such criterion must depend eventually on what the artist intends.

What about the really outlandish cases? Suppose an artist paints a cow and names it 'Derby winner 1979'. Are we then to say that it really is a representation of a horse, but not a very good one? The obvious conclusion to draw, if the artist is manifestly in his senses, is that the whole affair is a joke, or that perhaps the artist is satirizing the concern of the racing fraternity for fatstock prices rather than equestrianism? Whatever conclusion we draw, we must take i+ that the representation is of a cow, and that the artist intended it as such. For the product of an activity which requires so much skill and care over a period of some time can hardly be other than intended: such an outcome will not be a mere accident. What the artist does reveals his intentions as much as what he says.

In normal circumstances we expect the claim that a picture represents a certain object to be fleshed out by pointing to the features in the picture which correspond to various features of the object. (These are his ears, and this is his nose.) Where the correlations are detailed we may be able to draw information from the picture about the object. But the fact that we can do this does not guarantee that the likeness is a good one. As Goodman points out, from a picture in complementary colours we can draw a great deal of information about the object if the correlations hold. Equally a painting which distorts in a systematic way may yet allow information about its object to be drawn by the viewer, providing he knows the principles lying behind the distortion. In neither case, could we say that we have a good likeness. What then does make a good likeness?

A Good Likeness
If a picture is a good likeness then the object it pictures

must exist: the object of the picture needs thus more than a merely intentional existence. In these circumstances what a picture is like may be a criterion as to what a picture represents. A physiognomy as distinctive and as familiar as that of Churchill's enables us to guess easily that a particular picture is a picture of Churchill; even then, of course, it is not beyond the bounds of possibility that what we took to be a picture of Churchill is really a picture of an Albanian chieftain. Though a criterion, likeness is not a condition, for as we have seen it is not resemblance which makes x a picture of y.

Philosophical inquiries best begin with problems. What then is the problem about understanding what it is for a picture to be a good likeness? It can be set up in terms of a puzzling anecdote in the history of painting, an anecdote which is presumably apocryphal, since a not dissimilar story was told about Giotto. I am going to call it the Zeuxis problem. It was said that his representations were so life-like that even the birds of the air were deceived and tried to peck the painted fruit. Yet he was upstaged by Parrhasios in the creation of greater verisimilitude. Now the interesting point is that we, from our vantage point in the history of art, would not describe the paintings of Giotto as exceptionally realistic or faithful to the appearances. They are very great art, of course, and represent, as the cliché goes, a new humanity in the art of the period. But they hardly exemplify what philosophically naïve writers sometimes call photographic realism. The naïve view is that the ability to represent the appearances is a matter of gradually acquired skill and that, at any point in the history of art, its public could immediately measure the degree of verisimilitude reached. But if the history of art is a history of increasing technological competence in which the failings of any attempt at representation were immediately obvious, then it is hard to see what we should make of these anecdotes. Whether they are true or not is unimportant, what matters is that they were told and were, possibly, propaganda in favour of one artist by his supporters. What the Zeuxis problem suggests is that a direct comparison between picture and object disclosing the degree of verisimiltude is itself relative to certain standards of a good likeness – standards which vary over time.

There are two models which may help us to make sense of the concept of a good likeness; if we stress the role of convention then it is natural to see language as an analogy; if we think of painting as a form of technology, then photography may offer a more striking comparison. Let us first suppose that pictures are good or bad likenesses in the way that statements are true or false. Pictures denote as statements represent states of affairs or words objects: they represent through conventions. There is, first of all, one striking dissimilarity between the two cases; we can number the elements in a sentence which is used to make a statement; it may consist of six or so words, twenty or thirty characters, or whatever. But there is no clear basis for enumerating the elements of a picture. There is no convention which tells us that we should start counting the brush-strokes from the top left. But this disanalogy is less serious than others which render the model useless. A picture can be a good, bad or mediocre likeness. An artist could do two passable sketches of a sitter one of which might be a better likeness than the other. But no sense can be attached to the idea that one statement can be more true than another. The logic of statements is two-valued. A still more damaging objection is the familiar criticism that picturing has no place for the assertion function. There is a syntactical basis in language for distinguishing assertions from denials, command or questions. But there is no clause built into Constable's picture of Flatford Mill which says 'This is how appearances are' any more than the assertion 'This is how appearances are not' is built into Matisse's portrait of his wife. But if pictures make no assertions, they are neither true nor false.

What the model does find a place for, however, is the way conventions play a role in pictorial representation. It is sometimes thought by protagonists of the idea of technological progress that the discovery of perspective gave us the technique which allows us to transcribe the visual experience of three-dimensional objects on to a two-dimensional plane. If we make a construction on the basis of light rays drawn from the subject to the eye of the viewer via a reticulated plane (as in the famous Dürer wood-cut) the artist, drawing on squared paper of the size of the frame which separates him from the model, will produce an accurate likeness given the required competence. Thus the competent draughtsman will ensure that the representation on the sheet, if drawn on tracing paper, will match the image seen in that, when held against the reticulated frame the outlines all coincide.

There are some familiar problems to do with perspective. When we see a façade consisting of columns, we do not see those at the ends as apparently thicker than those in the middle (given that their real thickness is the same). Yet if drawn according to perspective those at the ends of the façade will appear wider than those in the centre. The reason is that the eye is closer to the centre and therefore lines drawn from the eye to each side of the column will form tangents on the column in such a way as to disclose less than half the surface, whereas those at the end reveal half their surface. Now normally we scan a façade and thus do not compare the relative width of columns as we can do in a picture, and so we are unaware of this. Thus a picture painted in strict accordance with the laws of perspective may be a distortion of how an object appears to the human eye. The form of reproduction of a visual field which apparently by-passes the problems of the draughtsman's competence, is, of course, photography and this is the second of the two models which I described as possibly helping us to understand the concept of a likeness. Let us then assume that a picture is a good likeness of an object if it matches a photograph taken from the position at which we take the artist to have been standing at the time he painted the picture. Two negatives, one of the scene and one of the picture of the scene may be laid one on top of the other. To the extent the outlines coincide the picture is a faithful representation, a good likeness. Not only does this second analysis use the idea of a photograph in teasing out the content of the concept of a good likeness but it sets up the photograph as the ideal representation of the object. This approach to verisimilitude in representation is at least as old as photography itself.

Problems of perspective do not, however, disappear. We are familiar with the fact that a billiard ball held close to the lens appears enormously inflated. Such techniques have been used in record sleeve designs recently. Conversely, it has been remarked that there is nothing like a camera for turning a mountain into a molehill. A photograph does not coincide with how things appear. Even if we set this aside there are other problems, as we shall now see.

To return to the Zeuxis problem,[7] the photography model naturally sorts with that view of the history of art which sees it as a form of technology in which artists gradually developed the skill to record appearances; it is a view which appealed to Constable amongst many other artists. Constable viewed painting as a form of science. Then we can well imagine that a sudden revolution in artistic style, such as the grasp of perspective, foreshortening, *sfumato* or highlighting might so impress an artist's contemporaries as to lead to the sort of exaggerated claim embodied in the fables that contemporaries related about Zeuxis and Giotto. Combining the view of the history of art as a matter of technological progress with the ideal of photographic realism, the invention of photography will seem like a *deus ex machina* which rendered obsolete the attempt to capture more and more accurately the look of things.

Of course, achieving a coincidence of outline in the way I suggest is only half the battle. If the photograph is in black and white then the colours have to be translated into tone. Early photographs rendered reds and yellows as dark tone and blue and violet as light; even in the panchromatic film developed later, red and green tend to be represented by the same value. And the problems of catching and matching colour in colour photography are familiar even to the amateur.

The photographer has a choice of lens at his disposal

which can mitigate the effects of apparent distortion of the visual image, but it needs to be stressed that there is no way of photographing such that the photographic image automatically accords with the image the eye receives. Spots of sunlight reflected in water appear as spots on a short exposure but as streaks to the eye. So the choice of exposure time is another decision the photographer must make. The number of choices the photographer has to make, let alone the special techniques of multiple exposure, retouching, etc., which have been available since its early days, make it hard to see why photography should ever have been considered a purely mechanical means of transmitting an image, and thus a uniquely accurate rendering of what the eye sees. Nevertheless, critics of photography from the nineteenth century onwards attacked it on the grounds that it left no room for the use of imagination and sensibility. These criticisms have been recently revived by Dr Roger Scruton.[8] Scruton presents a conception which he calls 'ideal photography' in which the causal connection between object and image recorded on light sensitive paper is untouched by human hand; in this ideal case there is no question of retouching, employing composite photographs, or cutting up and reassembling the photographs, or any of the other techniques normally used. He does not even envisage the selection of lens, camera angle or subject matter. 'Ideal photography' is not polluted with the aims and methods of painting. Of course, as Scruton is well aware, the class of ideal photographs is a class with no members. At the very least the photographer must point the camera and operate the shutter.

What is, I think, puzzling is why Scruton, and other writers less explicitly before him, should think that 'ideal photography' represents the essence of photography. Certainly there have been movements in the history of photography towards what he calls 'ideal photography'; the 'straight photography' movement of Stieglitz and Strand is the most famous example, but such a movement was itself an artistic movement. It as much incorporates an artistic decision within a certain photographic tradition as the decision of a painter to ride a bicycle across his canvas and take what comes. Indeed, a good name for this particular sort of aesthetic movement might be minimum action photography; the photographer achieves his effect by doing the minimum, pointing the camera and operating the shutter rather than by elaborately arranging the model, retouching, sophisticated lighting, and so on. Such practices are not to be set against artistic practices, they are themselves artistic practices within a tradition.

For Scruton, the photographer does not do enough in the production of the photograph for it to merit being called a representation. It incorporates less and less of the photographer's conception of the character of what he is photographing the closer it approaches 'ideal' photography. The normal practices of photographers in colouring and altering in various ways the negatives or prints only indicate that photography is a sort of bastard painting, and not an art in its own right.

Although the pejorative overtones are unmerited, it is, I think, undeniable that photography does not seem to be a distinct art form in the way that music, painting or drama are. To some extent this can be seen in the critical approach we adopt; we look for the same virtues of balance in design and composition as we expect from a good painting. Of course, the informed judge will also know all about the special techniques available to the photographer, but the availability of such special techniques does not in itself make photography a new medium anymore than the fact that the informed judge of contemporary music needs to know about the novel electronic sounds available which makes the music of Stockhausen a different art form. On balance I would have thought that the generic nature of the responses to photography and painting are sufficiently similar for us to regard them as sibling arts. It is worth remarking that, in the case of the cinema, not only are the techniques very different (for montage, cutting, wiping, fading and dissolving are not found in any other art) but the techniques are perceptible to the audience. It is hard for the non-expert to tell if a photograph has been retouched or is a composite print, and I dare say that even the expert may sometimes go astray. But the point about montage and the other techniques is that they are techniques of editing that are supposed to be visible to the audience. They are not merely not hidden from the audience but they also form part of the work of art, and not merely part of its production, they are means by which the director can, without any hint of deception, draw his audience's attention to what he wishes to emphasise and, through this, use the film to embody what he wishes to express.

What underlines this considerable difference between the film and other arts is the extent to which film, unlike photography, has formed a tradition of works in relative isolation from the other arts. Whereas photography has always looked to the visual arts for its models, film makers have been influenced by earlier film makers thus forming a tradition of film making which is updated by each new development in the art of the film. The Scottish pioneers in portrait photography, Hill and Adams, deliberately imitated the style of the Dutch masters. Later we see the influence of the pre-Raphaelites in Julia Cameron's work. Photography has not created a repertoire of devices, a tradition or internal history which characterises the art; it has too frequently turned to art for its models. Conversely, the influence of photography on art was very great indeed. There are the obvious cases such as Muybridge's studies of horses in motion which showed the 'flying gallop' position to be a fiction. It is almost certain that Ingres used photographs in his self-portraits because those painted after the invention of the daguerrotype show a mole on his left cheek and those after show it on his right, exactly as if he painted first from a mirror image and then from a photograph. But the more interesting influences are Corot's massing of light and shade into large undifferentiated areas; since early photographs were not sensitive to subtle differences in light this stylistic feature very likely shows their influence.

Film has much more distinctive and independent styles; we can date a film from its style as easily as we can date poetry. The debts of film directors are generally to other directors, if there are exceptions, then they are exceptions. Any good film criticism immediately confirms the proposition that film derives from film and that the tradition is as closed a one as that of any other art.

What painters paint depends upon what previous painters have painted; somebody once said that a painter paints a tree not because he has seen one, but because somebody else has painted one. Eighteenth-century painters painted lakeland because its scenery reminded them of Claude and Poussin. Constable saw his landscapes in terms initially dictated by Gainsborough, and Gainsborough before him in terms of the earlier Dutch landscape masters. Gombrich describes the situation as one of schema and correction; each great master adds to and modifies the conventions of his predecessors; by doing this he adds to the conventions upon which his successors can draw. This can be seen very graphically in the drawing manuals which passed down the techniques acquired by earlier generations of artists. Their modern descendants are such familiar publications as 'How to Draw Cats' and 'How to Draw Birds'. Viewed in this light the distinction between symbol and representation becomes less clear. One shades into another; some of the schema available in earlier centuries may seem to us extremely stylised.

I do not think there is any straight forward answer to the problem posed by the Zeuxis anecdote. It is certainly true that we accept a measure of convention in visual representation of which we are at times unaware.

However, if we concur with Goodman[9] that representation is entirely a matter of convention, then we lose the right to argue that some conventions produce better likenesses than others. Do we not want to say that the invention of perspective or highlighting enabled artists to produce better likenesses? Most of us, I think, would. We would also think that Goodman's thesis leaves unanswered the question as to why, at least up to the turn of the century, such 'inventions' were accepted and put to use if it was not for the fact that the conquest of the appearances became that much closer. We may look at a painting and pay close attention to the conventions which it obeys. An art historian studying the style of French seventeenth-century art might, through his professional interests, be more concerned with the conventions than with the subject matter. In the same way I may look at a theatrical performance taking in the conventions of dramatic presentation, the proscenium arch or the apron stage, or the conventions of soliloquy. On the other hand, I may, as it were, see through the conventions and view the representation directly, and it is in these circumstances that theatrical or dramatic illusion is more likely to take place. Now to an extent these two approaches are independent of the artificiality or otherwise of the conventions of the particular mode of representation. Familiarity with a set of conventions may well enable us to see through these conventions at the representations as a representation of an object.

No doubt this explains the puzzling fact that a chimpanzee was able to recognise a photograph of a chimpanzee, but photographs of themselves shown to primitive people were not recognised as depictions. Its explanation lies in the fact that human beings already have representational conventions, and animals do not; for them photographs are not puzzling (or perhaps they mistake them for the real thing). However we can, once a measure of sophistication has been obtained, suspend or bracket off the perspective which we usually 'read through' just as, when reading proofs, we pay attention to print which we usually 'read through'. The artist relies on his expectation that his public will read the lines he draws in a particular way; this enables them to pay attention to the object represented. But we can, if we choose, concentrate on the conventions of depiction.

At any one time, a particular style may be quotidian as far as the public is concerned. This is certainly true in other arts; for instance in music the accepted harmonic language is that of the Viennese classical school as far the average music lover is concerned. Equally, I suppose, for the purchaser of prints in departments stores, the Impressionists are slightly daring and the artist who paints the landscape 'as it is' is, *par excellence*, Constable. But, no doubt, the history of philistine taste remains to be written.

As artistic revolutions show, an adjustment of the conventions of depiction may make it possible to catch certain elements in the appearance which were formerly impossible. The modification of schemata of depiction is not necessarily gradual. Then the artist who engineered the change may be greeted as Giotto was. But we should not conclude that members of the previous generation were necessarily aware of the gap between their representational conventions and what really constituted a good likeness. They would also have judged some of their contemporaries as more realistic artists than others. This impression of verisimilitude will become further entrenched by the ways in which we tend to see objects in ways influenced by artist's representations. Thus it is not as though we can compare with a painting a view of reality uninfluenced by conceptions of what things look like. Essentially this takes the form of directing what we notice and what we pay attention to. We notice landscapes and features of landscapes which fit ideals drawn from the paintings of Constable, Wilson or Palmer. No doubt on occasion photographs are accepted as good likenesses to the extent that they cohere with the conventionally accepted representations of the object depicted. However, I have also quoted Scharf's evidence that photography also changed those conventions. So the mastery of the appearances was hard won. Each addition to the repertoire of devices for representation, the painting of spokes in motion, the sculpting of a turning torso or the representation of the veins and ligaments of a limb may well have so astonished an artist's contemporaries as to lead to the Zeuxis fable with the implication that *trompe l'oeil* effects were the mark of realism. The eye is neither purely innocent nor entirely corrupted by artistic styles and the inventory of representational devices. The ordinary man learns from the artist how to see things and what things are worth painting. But he does not lose the capacity to judge the relative accuracy of different modes of representation though he may, when he is not deliberately paying attention to these conventions take a representation produced in harmony with them as naturalistic. But this presumes that the conventions are familiar and accepted.

Literature and Representation

'A great writer creates a world of his own and his readers are proud to live in it' (Cyril Connolly). There is no exact parallel in literature to the problems we have just been considering. As far as the general doctrine of representation is concerned, however, a long tradition sees this as the task of writers. Samuel Johnson,[10] for instance, argues that it is the function of literature to represent not the particular but the general. Of Shakespeare he writes,

His characters are not modified by the customs of particular places, unpractised by the rest of the world; by the peculiarities of studies or professions, which can operate but upon small numbers; or by the accidents of transient fashions or temporary opinions: they are the genuine progeny of common humanity, such as the world will always supply, and observation will always find . . .

. . . The event which he represents will not happen, but if it were possible, its effects would probably be such as he has assigned; and it may be said, that he has not only shewn human nature as it acts in real exigencies, but as it would be found in trials, to which it cannot be exposed.

A regard for these merits in a writer has been frequently admixed with the view that the function of literature is to imitate the ideal: what a poem describes in Sidney's[11] words, is 'better than nature bringeth forth'; a parallel in the visual arts is provided by Vasari's emphasis on the way a sculptor can improve upon nature' by creating an ideal figure to which nothing in reality exactly corresponds. Such a view of the task of art leads, quite naturally, to the censorship of those literary works which do not promote moral advancement by holding before us an image of the ideal. One of its descendants is, beyond question, socialist realism, which assigns to the artist the task of improving the consciousness of the masses.

Either the imitation of actual general characteristics or of the ideal is compatible with that most prevalent of modern theories, the view that literature creates an imaginary world in which we may see reflected the manners and modes of the world in which we live, but in which the individuals are distinct inventions with no parallels in our actual world. Of the benefits of training the imagination by reading few are in doubt, moral philosophers least of all. Shelley's dictum has become a cliché:

A man, to be greatly good, must imagine intensely and comprehensively: he must put himself in the place of another and of many others: . . . the great instrument of moral good is the imagination.

Fiction gives us a means by which we may share the private mental life of possible if not actual people. These experiments equip us to share imaginatively the life of our fellow men.

Bearing this in mind, we may now turn to a recent form of a representationalist theory of literature.[12] To Liebniz we owe the concept of 'possible worlds'; logically necessary propositions are those propositions which are true in all possible worlds as against factual truths which merely record what is true of this world. Since a factual proposition like 'Birds nest in the spring' is not true of necessity, we can say that it is possible that the facts which this proposition describes could have been different. The Leibnizian way of putting this would be to say that there is a possible world in which birds do not nest in the spring but that possible world is not our actual world. By contrast, 'triangles are three-sided' is a necessary truth and therefore true in all possible worlds. Recent work in modal logic has made use of the theory in order to discuss such diverse topics as reference and the nature of the laws of physics. Given its present ubiquity as a philosophical nostrum, it is unsurprising that enthusiasts have found imaginative literature a suitable target. Thus a novel can be thought of as describing a possible world which differs from our own in that the individuals in it do not exist in ours. More pertinently the special qualities of imaginative fiction can be identified; to any meaningful question about a matter of fact in our world there is an answer even if we do not know what it is; either there are green men on Saturn or there are not; however there is no answer to the question 'How many children has Lady Macbeth?'. The fictional Sir Joseph Porter, KCB of *H.M.S. Pinafore* has unnumbered sisters, cousins ('he reckons them in dozens') and aunts and to the question how many they number there is no answer: however there is an answer to the question how many female relatives the real life personage who was being pilloried, W.H. Smith, actually had.

To descend to yet more detail, how is it that we can say that it is true that Lady Macbeth is married and false that Mr Chadband is (was?) a bachelor? Neither proper-name designates an actual individual past or present. (The temptation to describe them as existing in the past is seductive and suggests that we tend to think of fiction as a sort of history; to an extent it is when we are gripped by this illusion that we are moved by the fate of fictional characters.)

There is, of course, a classical account of how we can describe non-existent individuals and it is to be found in Russell's Theory of Descriptions. Russell was exercised by the problem of analysing propositions like 'The King of France is bald' given that there is no King of France. If we say that the proposition is false we appear to commit ourselves to the proposition that the King of France is not bald, when what we wish to deny is that the King of France exists. The details of the argument do not concern us here. Suffice to say that Russell treats such a pro-position as a compound of existential and predicative statements, giving 'There is one and only one person now reigning over France, and there is no one now reigning over France who is not bald.' (There are alter-native formulations.) Now since a conjunction is false if just one of its members is false, the above conjunctive compound statement is false. Applying this to fictional propositions, an example such as 'Lady Macbeth was married' now becomes a conjunction of 'There was a Lady Macbeth' (or some equivalent formulation) with a predicative proposition 'Lady Macbeth was married' and the whole can be declared false because there is no Lady Macbeth.

However the results of applying Russell's theory are not helpful. What we want to say is that 'Lady Macbeth was married' is true (when compared with Lady Macbeth was not married) and not false as Russell's analysis decrees. The results of the Russellian analysis run counter to our intuitions on the matter.

An alternative approach would be to follow the suggestion of Strawson and treat the statement as involving the relation of presupposing. Thus 'All John's children are in bed' presupposes, according to Strawson, that John has children, and the presupposition behind 'Lady Macbeth was married' is that there was a Lady Macbeth. But the exchange of a conjunction for a presuppositional relation, far from solving the problem, merely emmeshes us in fresh issues. The exact nature of presupposition and its difference from implying and entailing has long foxed philosophers of language; but there is a more pressing difficulty. We are invited to treat fictional statements as making presuppositions which we know to be false but which we allow, or make believe, for the fun of it. Once the allowance is made, and it does not have to be so crudely signalled as to start with 'Once upon a time', the story can proceed. But unless we can fill out 'make-believe', we are left with no way of choosing between 'Mr Chadband was married' and 'Mr Chadband was not married' for the truth or falsity of neither can arise. Even if, improbably, a character with that name and having those characteristics and adventures did exist, unbeknown to Dickens, the proposition 'Chadband was married' still is not true since that was not the character that Dickens named. He did not refer 'accidentally' to a real-life character of whose existence he was unaware. We can see, therefore, the attractions of possible world theory because we then can say that in the fictional world created by Dickens, if not in our actual world, it is true that Chadband was married. 'It is true that Chadband was married' then becomes elliptical for 'In the possible world corresponding to Dickens' fiction, Chadband was married'.

Before examining the relationship between the character of fiction and the fiat of the author, this is perhaps then the place to consider the problem of fictional counter-factuals, namely, statements of the form 'If Lear had not demanded proofs of his daughters' love, he would not have suffered as he did'. These counter-factuals are by no means frivolous. Even if propositions like these are not consciously considered by the reader, they form a background to his understanding of the work. What happens in a work of the imagination is connected to what has previously happened in the fiction in a way which must, if the fiction is intelligible, parallel the connections between events in the actual world. The events in a fiction are not just a necklace of events strung together; the connection between them must be of the order which would obtain had that possible world been the actual world. In David Lewis' words the difference between them must be 'minimal' for otherwise we lose both the intelligibility and the aesthetic point of fiction. A sympathetic and intelligent reading of the work requires a feeling for the inter-play of the actual and the possible. Anna Karenina lives in nineteenth-century Russia; real cities are mentioned and described; if she takes a train to St Petersburg then we know that it is a journey of several hours. Furthermore, her eventual suicide must be related to our conception of the sort of woman she is. The significance of this is sufficiently obvious to enable Dickens to make humorous use of it. Readers may recall Mr Crummles' theatre company in *Nicholas Nickleby*.

The plot was most interesting. It belonged to no particular age, people or country, and was perhaps the more delightful on that account, as nobody's previous information could afford the remotest glimmering of what would ever come of it.

Lewis has recently suggested a treatment of fictional propositions which is close to the account he gives of the more straightforward forms of counter-factuals long familiar to philosophers of science, (Statements of the form, 'If you were to strike this match it would ignite'.) A fictional proportion is acceptable if that possible world in which it is true is minimally different from that possible world which is our actual world. Now our world might not have been just as it is. Had I not been born, or had any of the readers of this book not been born, then the world would have been different from what it is. However you and I were born, and a world in which we do not exist remains only a possible world and not the actual world. There is only one actual universe but an infinity of possible universes. Amongst such possible universes are those universes in which the events recounted in *Anna Karenina* actually happened. To each work of imaginative fiction there corresponds a possible world; such a possible world differs from our own actual world only in what the author specifies. In all other respects the possible world corresponds with the actual.

In many ways this analysis does do justice to our reading of fiction. We assume that Mr Chadband has two arms and two legs because Dickens does not tell us otherwise. We assume that once Gloucester's eyes are put out he cannot see, because Shakespeare has not specified any miracles in the narrative of *Lear*. We take the fictional world to be different from our own only in the ways which the author has pointed out. The suppositions he makes are necessarily limited. It would be an impossible, indeed an endless, task to specify a world which touched in no ways our own. If, *per impossibile*, that task were completed the ensuing narrative could not comment on our world nor touch our sympathies and affections.

We can extend this account of fictional propositions to deal with fictional counter-factuals by allowing that just as a fictional world differs from our actual world only in certain respects, so the fictionally counter-factual world differs from the fictional world only in certain respects, though it is now at two removes from actuality. In both cases we fill in our picture of the possible world in question by making the assumption that the world differs minimally from its neighbour. We can thus treat the two problems of fictional propositions and fictional counter-factuals in tandem and this is what, from now on, I shall do.

Now, as Lewis himself points out, certain adjustments are required in this theory. There are counter-factuals which do not behave in quite the way this theory predicts. On the assumption that the world in question differs only minimally from our own, the counter-factual 'This dragon, were it to be irritated, would bite and scratch the opposition' would be true, rather than the counter-factual 'This dragon, were it to be irritated, would incinerate the opposition'. The analysis needs to be amended with a reference to the general conventions which obtain in a genre, and which underpin any particular fictional narrative. Dragons are defined as fire breathing because that assumption is a convention of the genre in which they appear. So the possible world departs from our actual world only in the respects specified by the author, and in whatever respects are specified by the conventions to which the fiction adheres. However, even then a difficulty remains; writers frequently aim to change conventions. We misread *Don Quixote* if we read it as a typical chivalric romance. The effect of the detail specified by the author is to produce a clash with the conventions of the genre to which the fiction apparently belongs.

Yet a further caveat must be that the commonplaces which we share with each other will be different from the common beliefs which unite author and readers at other times and in other societies. Understanding Milton requires knowing and understanding that corpus of beliefs and the areas of controversy over political and theological matters which are the background to the epics. Lewis sees that to understand what could be fictionally true in *Macbeth* requires knowing what beliefs Shakespeare's audience had about witches, the succession of monarchs, and so on. What is equally true, and what he does not seem to see, is that a writer at a time of theological or intellectual turmoil, such as Milton or Brecht, may have beliefs specific to a single sect or even to himself alone. The elements of anti-Nomianism and mortalism in Milton scandalised many of his contemporaries, and they would have read him with these in mind. Thus an accurate description of the possible world of *Paradise Lost* and the indicatives and the counterfactuals true of it may require knowledge of very specific beliefs. Lewis' final form of his thesis runs roughly as follows. A fictional proposition is true if those possible worlds in which it is told as known fact differs minimally from that world which is one of the collective belief worlds of the community of origin of the fiction. The reference to possible worlds incorporates the plural because the fiction may be less than specific about the precise denizens. (Since we do not know how many sisters, cousins and aunts Sir Joseph Porter has in *H.M.S. Pinafore*, the plural form is preferred since it allows as many possible worlds as there may be sisters, cousins and aunts.) This reflects one of the points we made earlier, namely that whereas realists assume that each question we can ask about the world has an answer, to the questions raised about a fiction there may be no answer. Whereas there is an answer to the question as to how many nieces or nephews a pope has, there is no answer to the question how many Sir Joseph Porter, KGB has. In fact the plural form is indispensable if we are to deal with dramatic productions in the same way. For a production of *Hedda Gabler* may be repeated every night for a week, on each night of which Hedda dies by shooting herself. If the world thus created is single then it is either impossible, or requires a nightly miracle of resurrection built into the play's background. Given that the possible world is not being described as in a fiction but presented, we require the proviso that each time *Hedda* is performed then a similar but not identical possible world is being presented. Consequently, we can see that the yokel who shoots Iago does not affect the work of art but simply prevents a particular token of that type 'X's interpretation of Iago being instantiated. There is a causal gap between us and the work which makes the work immune from our actions.

Now non-realists like Dummett who insist that the conditions for the truth of a proposition are related to our ability to acquire and use a language do not willingly acquiesce in the existence of truths which lie beyond our capacity to frame conditions for their warranted assertion. Dummett's familiar example is 'Jones was brave' asserted of a man, now dead, who never encountered danger. If there is no reason to think such propositions either true or false then one can ask a question such as 'Was Jones Brave?' of a man who existed in the real world, and to this question there is no answer. Therefore we cannot distinguish a fictional from a non-fictional history on the basis that an answer must exist for any question that can be asked about the latter but not the former.

Contrariwise fiction whose character is made dependent upon certain conventions makes it possible to answer any question that can be raised. I shall call this the Lieutenant Kije counterexample. In Prokofiev's eponymous ballet, the Czar mishears a reference to an officer, and thinks that a Lieutenant Kije is being referred to. Unwilling to correct the Czar, the officers make up a story about the young officer. Unfortunately the Czar takes an interest in Lieutenant Kije and eventually, to forestall embarrassment, the officers arrange to have him 'killed' and buried with military honours. Despite the fictional character of the story within the ballet, any question that the Czar asked was provided with an answer. The example is not entirely preposterous; Jane Austen was prepared to make up answers to questions from correspondents who asked what Elizabeth Bennet's favourite colour was. (The answer was 'blue'.) Now we can easily imagine a body of authors in charge of, perhaps, an epic. When one dies, a replacement is elected. When any question is asked about what any character was doing before the action started or when he was not 'on stage', the guild is empowered to answer.

The answers given have, of course, to be consistent with what has already been said, and here there may be difficulties. Indeed many, perhaps even most, fictional characters are inconsistently characterised whereas nothing in the real world can have inconsistent properties. A famous example occurs in *La Bête Humaine* where Zola describes the same night as 'a warm June night' and 'a sultry July night' — not so much a possible as an impossible world. Though this may seem the most trivial form of nit-picking, it is important to note what is wrong with Lewis' recommendation for dealing with it, for it leads us directly to the essence of fiction. He recommends that we decide what properties the fictional character 'really' has upon considerations drawn from the rest of that possible world. That is, by our informed fiat, the events are deemed to have taken or not to have taken place in June according to which seems to fit in best. Such a decision is exactly what the author makes in settling the characters of his fiction. Dickens decided what features Mr Chadband possessed and what he did not decide Mr Chadband did not possess. If an analogy is to be sought it is, as Iris Murdoch remarks, in the relation of God to His creation. The difference is that because the fictional characters are not fully described, they remain incomplete. Of which fictional characters do we know how often they cut their toenails? So the truth of a proposition about a fictional character depends upon its either being what was stated or entailed by what the author has stated. *Vox auctoris, vox dei.* But no critic or reader can usurp this function in the way Lewis suggests. The impossible world remains impossible.

There is, after all, a possible world in which Chadband was unmarried as well as the possible Dickensian world in which he was married, and when we say that it is true that Chadband is married we refer to the fictional world which Dickens created; without this we cannot say whether the proposition is true or false. The reference to the author is thus essential.

Possible world talk emerges very naturally out of what writers and critics say about fiction — witness the epigraph which commences this section. Yet when we lean on the notion it proves a rather treacherous crutch. The proposed treatment of dramatic performance and of the incompleteness of fiction seem to me unintuitive and the problems of inconsistent fiction not easily surmountable. However, alternative accounts in terms of 'make-believe' look either false or boring or both, and at least the possible world analysis gives us a way of raising important philosophical questions. The problem is that a similar device is needed to deal with the problems which arise from two authors writing different fictions about the same character and here, I think, the difficulties become both familiar and terminal. We cannot allow that Marlowe and Goethe are writing merely about two similar characters both named Faust. Yet such a conclusion is demanded if they are both specifying possible worlds. But the two fictions are about the same character, but ascribe to him different imaginary adventures. The problems derive from the ever-present temptation to think of possible worlds in realist terms, instead of considering the jargon as elliptical for talk of possible or imaginary characters and adventures.

It is an illuminating metaphor — though no more — to speak of a writer as creating a world. Some writers and dramatists seem better able to achieve this impression than others. Conrad's *Nostromo* creates such an extraordinarily vivid impression of a South American republic where life in its variety is lived behind the pages of the novel that we are not at all surprised when Tillyard gives a map. The opening of the final act of Puccini's *Turandot*, decently produced, wonderfully conveys the myriads of citizens of the great city of Peking uneasily awake. The impression can mislead; the writer creates an ordered world in which the loose ends of life are neatly tied. Henry James memorably spoke of the 'fatal futility of fact', contrasting it with the shape the novelist gives to a plot. Perhaps life might, as Hardy suggested, offer even more coincidences than fiction. It must, though, also be in many ways comparatively disordered. The plot of a novel must also be plausible, and Hardy did not excuse his novels of contrivance by the comparison with fact. As Aristotle remarked, a plausible impossibility is to be preferred to an implausible possibility.

The art of critical interpretation, to a discussion of which we shall soon move, is above all the art of bridging the fictional and the real world. The fiction presents us with an ordered world sufficiently near and yet sufficiently distant from our own to comment on it indirectly. We learn through fiction the reactions of possible individuals the exact like of whom we may never meet; yet the imaginative exercise of my sympathy increases what Aristotle called our fellow feeling, and Conrad our solidarity. The sense in which novels are sometimes said to be inductive picks out the way in which my understanding of my fellow men may be enhanced by my understanding of Leopold Bloom or Yossarian.

It would be an illusion to suppose that the novelist's picture of a world does not reflect his own values. But we do need to distinguish between those writers whose primary function is to advocate a certain view of society and those who either write from an unreflective sense of values or whose task is primarily critical. The difference is between the committed writer and others. No doubt a committed writer, a Marxist or a Catholic, or indeed a liberal, would argue that the second is merely a victim of false consciousness; he is unaware of or deceives himself about the function of an ideology which is quite as active as it is in the conscious propagandist. But here the idea that it is better to know yourself than to remain in ignorance seems to me to be highly dubious. Better a writer who writes in ignorance of the ideological tendencies of his work than one who grinds an axe.

The more explicitly a writer argues for an ideology and the more intrusive it is, the closer it verges upon propaganda. In Goethe's words *'So fühlt man Absicht und man ist Vestimmt'* (one sees the intention and is put off). In the writings of Lawrence and Shaw, the later plays of T.S. Eliot, or the late stories of Tolstoy, the reader is peculiarly conscious of an attempt to suborn him. It is natural to conclude that the less explicit the ideology the better for art. Consistently with this, David Caute has argued that in any ideological setting the imaginative writer sides with the individual against those social forces which threaten to crush him. The writer, the dramatist or the film-maker all have devices which enable us to identify with one individual, the hero of the narrative, against his enemies. But such a task for the writer is historically recent. The duties of the writer of the *Battle of Maldon* or of the bard in medieval Wales were to record the qualities and the achievements of his society and his patron. Cruttwell points out that hardly anyone in the circles that Donne moved in ever questioned the validity of a hierarchical view of society, the right of the grandee to receive the homage and deference of those below him was universally accepted, at least until the Commonwealth. It is anachronistic to see any sycophancy in that. But if a present-day poet laureate writes a poem in honour of a public figure, we cringe. At least since Marvell's *Horatian Ode* on the return of Cromwell from Ireland we expect a degree of irony and ambiguity in the relation of a poet to the powers that be.

I have written as though our historical imagination is unfettered. In fact, there are surely limitations on the range of writers with whom we can sympathise. Our literary taste is always likely to be more circumscribed than taste in music, architecture or design. Wayne Booth, in the *Rhetoric of Fiction*, produces some effective examples. The reader who does not value spontaneity as against the Puritan conscience is not going to make much of Henry James' *Ambassadors* nor will the Roman Catholic find as much in Milton as the Protestant. Marxists would be unsurprised at this. Their difficulty is the opposite one of explaining how we respond to as much literature as we do. Ernst Fischer argues that Marxism demands that the artist depict the rising society, and that the writer therefore needs to be aware of this social function. In a capitalist society the artist is free and alone, but in a socialist society he is in fundamental agreement with the direction in which it is evolving. The artist in a late bourgeois society neither speaks to nor on behalf of any large section of the people; the appeal of his art is limited and the works he produces are marketed by institutions which operate in much the way that they do in selling soap powders or washing machines. Art appeals more and more to the élite, and art objects are seen more and more as objects carrying a monetary value. Consequently, the artist shares in the alienation which typifies the modern capitalist work force. He creates objects for consumption by a public whose individual responses he cannot know, and the relation of the artist to his work converges on that of the factory worker. He still has incomparably greater power over the artefact, of course, and his work will find its public, if one exists, simply by elimination (though the same could be said of any other worker). The doctrine of art for art's sake is the apotheosis of this particular conception of the artist and his role.

The major problem remains for Marxist aestheticians. They believe that human nature changes as society, under the influence of economic changes, itself alters. Our interest in the art of the past thus becomes problematic. Does it not require a knowledge of the society in which it was produced in order to understand it? For art is part of the superstructure of society which is, at least in part, related to the economic base; the examples that Marxist writers on art use show very clearly that the art they admire is art which, like the novels of Dickens, both develops out of a particular society and comments critically on the mores and values of that society, thereby anticipating changes to a more equitable state.

But the art of a society very different from our own ought to present difficulties rather greater, it seems to me, than those we do encounter. Certainly, it is not easy for the Westerner to get the hang of Japanese fiction simply because the mores of the society are so very different, but the visual arts of other societies present less problems. Equally we might expect that the art of the West becomes less accessible the more distant it is in time from our own day. To some extent our experience

bears this out: Spenser is less accessible than Wordsworth. On the other hand, is not George Eliot or Dickens
more accessible than Joyce? Clearly there are many
factors at work here; some writers are simply more
difficult than others.

What the Marxist seems unable to recognise is one
factor which strikes me as extremely important in our
appreciation of the art of the past. That is our sense of a
common humanity. Part of the pleasure of reading
Horace is just in seeing how he expressed fears and
pleasures which are so like our own; suburbia threatens
the farmland of his childhood, and death looms before
the middle-aged poet; nothing can prevent the years
from flying past. Commonplaces apart, great literature
often does render articulate observations we have only
half-formed for ourselves; in Keats' marvellous phrase it
is 'almost a remembrance'. In D.H. Lawrence's *The Rainbow* a small girl tries to help her father in planting
potatoes. She plants them too closely

'Not so close', he said, stooping over her potatoes, taking out
some and rearranging the others. She stood by looking on,
with the painful terrified helplessness of childhood. He was so
unseeing and confident, she wanted to do the thing yet she
could not.

Powerless to help, she runs off to play beside a brook,
when her father nears her he says,

'You didn't help me much'.

The child looked at him dumbly. Already her heart was
heavy because of her own disappointment. Her mouth was
dumb and pathetic.

But he did not notice, he went his way.

And she played on, because of her disappointment persist-
ing even more in her play. She dreaded work, because she
could not do it as he did. She was conscious of the great breach
between them. She knew she had no power. The grown-up
power to work deliberately was a mystery to her.

As Johnson remarks in a different context, 'I have never
seen these notions in any other place; yet he who reads
them here persuades himself he has always felt them'.
Lawrence describes experiences which I suspect most

children have had. The pleasure of recognition merges into a sense of our common humanity with the writer who could set down such things, and of the continuity of our real world with this imaginative world. When art of the more remote past meets us in this way the recognition may be more of a shock, akin I suspect to the effect which old photographs can have upon us. Our relationship to the art of the past is a far more complex affair than Marxists can imagine: the similarity of human beings rather than differences in their consciousness is what sometimes strikes us. It is tempting to suppose that because this passage from *The Rainbow* is so touchingly convincing that it represents the truth. 'Isn't life just like that', we exclaim. But what sort of truth is being presented here? It is not that there was a real father called Will and a real daughter, Anna, and that this incident actually happened. It wouldn't make any difference, we feel, if there was and it had. Nor would it matter if Lawrence was describing real people and real incidents with the names and locations altered. (We know from Harry Levin's biography that he frequently did this.) What we feel can be better described as the impression that it would be both wholly in character and also revealing of character that Anna should react in this way. I cannot remember a similar incident in my childhood, though it now seems 'almost a remembrance' that I was aware of the extraordinary competence of adults and firmly believed that I could never achieve such competence; that it would one day be expected of me frightened me.

The 'problem of belief' has been hotly debated amongst writers on aesthetics. On the one hand, some have argued that it is always aesthetically irrelevant to consider the truth or falsity of the various propositions a work of literature contains. The structure of our experience of verse is such that we do not take into account the truth or falsity of propositions the verse contains. Thus in the couplet

> So well bred spaniels civilly delight
> in mumbling of the game they dare not bite.

the fact, and I take it to be a fact, that this is the way spaniels actually behave is of no consequence. R.J. Elliot, in a celebrated article, argues that in fact we admire this couplet not least because it 'states neatly and economically what is the case'. Plausible as this sounds, I do not think it withstands scrutiny. Suppose it was universally known that spaniels were really more like Dobermann pinschers or Dalmations, vicious and unreliable predators who will demolish a partridge as soon as look at it, but that it is a poetic convention that they are pliable gun dogs; alternatively it might be widely and erroneously believed that they are obedient and reliable, and Pope, as a breeder of dogs, alone knew the truth but chose the simile for its effect knowing how his literary public would take it. In neither case does the couplet lose its literary force.

It is, perhaps, more plausible to suppose that those propositions which are clearly presumed in a satire must be true for the satire to have the aesthetic effect it has. But again this succumbs to the most cursory inspection. We need to know that Swift was pillorying in early eighteenth-century English politics to respond to *Gulliver's Travels* but we do not need to know that his beliefs about it were true; they might have been very prejudiced, for all we know. The point of *Animal Farm* is lost if we do not know it is a satire, but we do not have to know that what Orwell believed about Stalinist Russia is true. So the way truth enters into an appreciation of literature is circuitous to say the least. Irony and satire do demand that we know the attitude of the author towards the object of the irony or satire so the question of truth enters there all right, but the balance of the argument rather favours Isenberg's claim that we set aside questions of truth when assessing the aesthetic effect of a passage.

The 'no-truth' theory, as it has been called, is, of course, cousin to that account of the aesthetic attitude which stresses disinterestedness; in both cases we are thought to abstract from considerations which are normally of the utmost relevance. But in leaning towards Isenberg I certainly would not wish to deny the Aristotelian claim that 'plausibility' counts. Providing we are wary, it does not do very much harm to consider that what a master does is to create an imaginary world or an imaginary society which has such recognisable resemblances to our own that we can empathise with and learn from the turmoils of its denizens. To correct Marianne Moore's famous aphorism, it depicts an imaginary toad in a real garden. It is true that often a fictional world closely corresponds to our world. Where it does not, as in much science fiction, the richness and depth of the fiction suffers.

We have considered some specific problems in the representative arts. Some general themes are, I think, beginning to emerge. Amongst these are the role both of critical interpretation and authorial intention in art and these topics will be more formally discussed in Chapter 5. First of all, however, we must ask whether a form of representationalism can be applied to an art like music which seems, at first sight, to resist a representationalist approach.

4

Expressionism

Of all the arts, music and architecture seem the least amenable to a representationalist theory of art. Paintings represent what they depict and a novelist produces a representation of whatever imaginary events he records as does the dramatist and film director. But it is hard to see what music represents. In exceptional circumstances a composer may imitate certain sounds which occur outside the concert hall, of course. Numerous pieces incorporate the major third of the sound of the cuckoo, and in the second movement of his *Pastoral Symphony* Beethoven quotes other bird songs. Honneger's *Pacific 231* and, even more effectively to my mind, Villa Lobos' *Little Train of the Caipira*, reproduce the sound of a steam train. But, as Charles Avison remarked, 'as an art music has very confined powers' and what powers it has are seldom used. Without extra-musical clues we would be hard put to tell whether the peroration of a Soviet symphony represents the victory of the workers or the capitalists.

Music, especially then, is a *prima facie* counterexample to a general representationalist account of the arts. To this we may react in one of two ways: either we may seek a way in which music does represent, or we may look for another general characterisation of the arts to replace representationalism. Both these alternatives have found supporters. Many writers have argued that music does represent, but that it does not so much represent the visible world as the inner workings of the mind. Music represents mental states. In particular, it has been often argued that music represents the emotions. From this it is but a short step to the idea that the composer expresses his emotion in the music. This is in turn but a special case of a theory which has commanded very general support, the Expressionist theory of art.

Expressionism in general can be seen as an alternative to representationalism as an account of what it is for an artefact to be a work of art. What marks out art as peculiarly different from the other products of human ingenuity is that in art the creator of the work expresses himself. In his monumental work on J.S. Bach, Albert Schweitzer begins by outlining just such an expressionist aesthetics. 'In reality the material in which the artist expresses himself is a secondary matter.' Music is only a hieroglyph in which are recorded the emotional qualities of the visions of the concrete imagination. This is but a variant of what is known to philosophers as the Croce-Collingwood or Idealist theory of art.[1] In the view of Collingwood, art involves a relationship between an image, idea, intuition or a concept of the work which exists initially in the creator's mind and its externalisation in the form of a poem, a piece of music, a painting or a play which is a public object which the audience can appreciate. The 'real' work of art, the work of art proper is the intuition in the creator's mind.

'Intuition' is Croce's term for the mental activity of the creator. Collingwood speaks of what the artist 'feels' or of the artist's 'emotion'; in 'art proper', he maintains, the artist 'makes a clean breast' of his experience and is an artist only in so far as his expression of his emotion is candid.

Two important caveats need to be made here. It would be natural to suppose that in externalising his intuition the artist was expressing it, expression being a public matter. After all, we think of expression in terms not only of speech but also gesture, grimaces etc. But, according to both Croce and Collingwood, nothing could be further from the truth. The intuition is the expression. The intuition may spring fully-armed into the head of the composer as it apparently did in the case of Mozart, or it may take weeks, months, even years to reach its final form. The consequence is that the creator cannot be sure of the form his intuition is going to take until it takes it. Unlike the craftsman, who knows in advance what he is going to do and whose work is therefore a means to an end, the artist does not plan and then execute the work. Once the 'plan' is complete the real work is done.

This theory of art, then, depends upon a sharp distinction being made between art and craft. The second mistake that the unwary might make is to suppose that the material on which the artist works is of any particular importance to the work of art *per se*. It is not. Externalisation is a matter of craft, and that craft can, of course, be learned, but as far as the work of art is concerned it is very much as a secondary matter; in Schweitzer's words 'the part of a work which is perceptible by the senses is in reality only the intermediate state between two active efforts of the imagination'. Collingwood would deny that the visible artefact is even part of the work of art. Now the objections to this form of expressionism are so obvious as to make its refutation almost a model exercise in philosophical method. Firstly, to describe the real work of art as the intuition of the artist involves an arbitrary and apparently pointless redefinition of the term. What do we gain from a definition of 'work of art' on the basis of which we have to say that the National Gallery contains no works of art at all? Secondly, the existence of these intuitions cannot be established; the only reason for supposing that they exist is the existence of the externalisation. So the concept has about as much utility as such ontologically fabulous beasts as 'volitions' and their explanatory value is equally slim. Thirdly, if these intuitions cannot be inspected, how can we be sure that the artist has successfully communicated his ideas to us? Can we distinguish between a very successful communication and one which is not quite so successful?

It has always seemed to its critics that the Idealist theory makes far too rigid a distinction between the intuition and the medium. Schweitzer writes as though the artist first has an idea and then looks about for a medium in which to present that idea. The charge, however, is less fair when brought against Croce and Collingwood. For

Croce, the capacity to externalise is a test of the vitality and clarity of the initial idea. But it is surely a just criticism of both forms of Idealism that, in fact, the medium itself suggests ideas to the creator? It has often been remarked that piano technique itself seems to suggest musical ideas to pianist-composers like Chopin, Liszt or Rachmaninov. On the other hand, it is certainly obscure, as Collingwood argues, as to what could count as the means whereby the poet creates his poem. The words are more properly parts of the poem than the means to its creation and the libretto of an opera is not the means by which the opera is created. If Collingwood is trading on a distinction between craft, in which the means are distinct from the created object, and art, then much the same problem can be raised with respect to craft. The wood ends up as part of the carpenter's table, after all, and it seems equally proper to query whether the lump of clay or block of wood are means to the production of the craft object. What something is made out of is not a means to its production. The point that Collingwood's thesis really depends upon is that the artist creates the work when he works it out in his head; once he has done this the creative act is complete. For all the emphasis on the interpretative task of performers and on the role of the audience, the impression remains that the difference between art and craft ultimately lies in a private mental act of the artist. Collingwood argues that where the aim is entertainment or the intention is to arouse certain emotions then what is created cannot count as art proper: the same is true when the purpose is religious or political. Thus on this theory, most of the great religious art of both western and eastern tradition do not count as art at all. In all these cases the work is being conceived as a means to an end.

It is wholly characteristic of Collingwood that he takes words which have an accepted usage and then uses them in a specialised way, maintaining all the while that he is merely using everyday expressions in their usual sense. Thus he holds that art which is merely designed to arouse pleasure in the listener or viewer is not art proper but merely 'amusement' or 'entertainment' art. Art which is designed to have an effect upon people, arousing their emotions in one way or another, he describes as 'magical art'. In his view, art may have coincidentally these features of giving pleasure or arousing emotion but it is not in virtue of these features that it counts as 'art proper'. In order to be 'art proper' it must not have an ulterior motive beyond the artist's expression of his emotion.

As Hospers remarks, the theory seems to require that we know a great deal about the inner workings of the minds of artists in the throes of creation. It is very implausible to suppose that until we can establish what went on in Leonardo's mind during the painting of the Last Supper we are in no position to say whether it is a work of art or not. The second criticism I would make is that a craftsman making a chair might equally well think through the conception of the chair prior to constructing it in precisely the way Croce and Collingwood require of art. But this would not make the construction of a chair a matter of art rather than craft. The distinction between the two is mislocated; in any case if we are to have a grasp of these concepts it must be in terms which can be employed by the ordinary observer; there must be public grounds for a distinction between art and craft. It cannot rest on an inner process which the artist alone can experience; certainly there seems little point in a redrawing of these concepts in the way that these philosophers advocate.

I began this chapter by suggesting that Expressionism could be seen simultaneously as a reaction to and as a form of representationalism. Collingwood would reject any form of representationalism because representation is a matter of skill and technique and thus belongs to craft. Of course a work of art may be representational, but it is not because of that that it is a work of art. Collingwood departs from Expressionism in at least one other way; in his view, art does not aim at arousing emotion. Until the artist has expressed it, he does not know what is being expressed so, at this level, no technique can be involved in expression. The artist creates a work of art as he works it out in his imagination and in the course of this the emotions are expressed. Although in this way his account is idiosyncratic it does share one important feature with what I shall call standard Expressionism. Both see the artistic process as consisting of the communicating of a private mental state to the public via the process of externalisation. Let us then now turn to 'standard Expressionism'.

The almost universal acceptance of the Expressionist theory of art can be illustrated from almost any branch of art in the last one hundred years. The rising pop star lisps his adherence to the doctrine, and it is a cliché of the Hollywood film biography where we see Schubert or Chopin strike his breast and rush to the piano. I have chosen to exemplify the doctrine from I. A. Richards' description of what he calls 'Tolstoy's infection theory of art'.

Mr Roger Fry, in his interesting Retrospect, records the shock with which Tolstoy's insistence upon communication struck contemporary students in England. 'What remained of immense importance was the idea that a work of art was not the record of beauty already existent elsewhere, but the expression of an emotion felt by the artist and conveyed to the spectator.' It will be useful to examine Tolstoy's account. He formulates his theory as follows: 'Art becomes more or less infectious in consequence of three conditions:
(i) In consequence of a greater or lesser peculiarity of the sensation conveyed.
(ii) In consequence of a greater or lesser clearness of the transmission of this sensation.
(iii) In consequence of the sincerity of the artist, that is, of the greater or lesser force with which the artist himself experiences the sensation which he is conveying.'[2]

Not every formulation of this view requires that the mental state being conveyed be an emotion. Tolstoy represents it as a thesis about the artist's sensation in the above gloss. There is evidently some uncertainty in Richards' mind as to precisely what mental states the artist conveys. On the one hand he quotes Roger Fry's reference to the emotion felt by the artist, and on the other hand he seems to concur with Tolstoy in describing it as a sensation. Now sensations and emotions are very different. I can have a sensation of nausea but it is not an emotion. It is equally implausible to suppose that to have the emotion of jealousy implies having a specific sensation, a 'jealousy-sensation', which accompanies it.

One striking fact about the arts is that we speak of them in quasi-personal terms. We can talk of music as being sad or cheerful, a painting or a poem may be gloomy. Now how can we justify the attribution of these 'mental' predicates to a work of art? A work of art is not sad in the way that a man is sad if he finds that his favourite ageratum has been eaten by slugs. Nor is it cheerful in the way that a young man may be cheerful on a Spring morning. So how can we explain the application of such terms?

The Expressionist theory does provide an answer, for it proposes that a work of art is sad or gay if the creator expresses his sadness in creating it, or his gaiety in creating it. So the theory kills two birds with one stone; it simultaneously answers the problem of how we can explain the application of mental predicates, and provides a theory which distinguishes works of art from other human artefacts. Unlike tables, chairs, aircraft and automobiles, works of art express their creators.

I shall begin by examining in detail the application of Expressionism to just one of the arts: music. There are good reasons for starting here. First, Expressionism has commanded such wide support amongst musicians as to have the status of the received theory. Secondly, a very influential statement of Expressionism, Deryck Cooke's *The Language of Music*[3] represents the most elaborate attempt I know at developing a detailed Expressionism with respect to a single art. However the criticisms I shall make can easily be generalised so as to provide a case against any form of Expressionism; amongst philosophers of art the theory is very much passé.

Aesthetic discussion of music has taken place within

fairly well-defined boundaries set by the analogy of language. Many writers over the past two centuries have defined their approach to the nature of music in terms of whether or not music is a language. The fundamental question has been answered in two ways; on the one hand, autonomists maintain that essentially music refers to nothing outside itself; the narratives of programme music or the occasional mimicry of outside sounds are irrelevant to its understanding. Stravinsky gave, perhaps, the most famous and uncompromising statement of the autonomist viewpoint:

For I consider that music is, by its very nature, essentially powerless to *express* anything at all, whether a feeling, an attitude of mind, a psychological mood, a phenomenon of nature etc. . . . *Expression* has never been an inherent property of music. If, as is nearly always the case, music appears to express something, this is only an illusion and not a reality. It is simply an additional attribute which, by tacit and inveterate agreement, we have lent it, thrust upon it, as a label, a convention – in short an aspect which, unconsciously or by force of habit, we have come to confuse with its essential being.

In the later *Expositions and developments*, Stravinsky modifies his view a good deal:

That over-publicised bit about expression (or non-expression) was simply a way of saying that music is supra-personal and supra-real and as such beyond verbal meanings and verbal descriptions. It was aimed against the notion that a piece of music is in reality a transcendental idea 'expressed in terms of' music, with the *reductio ad absurdum* implication that exact sets of correlatives must exist between a composer's feelings and his notation.[4]

On the other hand we have the heteronomist view that music does indeed refer to something outside itself; the most widely held form of this is the thesis that music is a language of the emotions, and is the view elaborated by Cooke in the book we are going to consider. For Cooke argues that the elements of music, melodic phrases, chords, harmonic progressions, etc., have an unambiguous emotional significance. He gives a lexicon, a glossary whereby predicates in the English language are matched with intervals, harmonic progressions and phrases of different shapes. Thus a rise from tonic to dominant through the major third expresses an outgoing optimistic note of joy and pleasure, whereas an ascending minor triad expresses pain and protest against misfortune. Descending from dominant to tonic through the major third expresses consolation, fulfilment, the feeling of having come home, whereas a similar descending progression through the minor triad expresses passive suffering, yielding to grief. Cooke elaborates on the significance of various phrases in this way.

What can be said in favour of the analogy between music and language? In many resepcts the analogy has as much in its favour and as much to be said against it as the analogy between language and pictures. It is hard to see that music could express propositions save by encoding them. If it were to do this it would be dependent upon an existing language for its meaning in a way which is true of no other language. For languages are independent of other languages, they do not require the existence of translation procedures into an existing language in order to secure meaning. Secondly, there seems no place for an assertion sign in musical notation or in performing conventions.

Even the much vaunted expressiveness of music may not tell in favour of the analogy. It is true that many writers have thought of music as the expressive art par excellence. Hanslick wrote,

Though all arts, without exception, have the power to act on our feelings, yet the mode in which music displays it is, undoubtedly, peculiar to this art. Music operates on our emotional faculty with greater intensity and rapidity than the product of any other art.[5]

But gesture and facial expression may equally be modes of expression and these are not linguistic in character. Indeed one nettle that advocates of Expressionism in music have not grasped is whether the expressive properties of music are to be considered as natural or as conventional signs. Whereas smoke is a natural sign of fire the word 'fire' is a conventional sign of fire. Guy Sircello has recently argued persuasively that expressions of emotion are natural signs caused by the mental states they express: my scowl is caused by the anger I feel and is a natural sign of that mental state. 'I feel irritated' is, on the other hand, a conventional sign. If I were a German, French or Welsh speaker I would use other words. Are we now to take an ascending minor triad as a natural or as a conventional expression of 'pain and protest against misfortune'? Oblivious of these problems, Cooke opts not so much for an analogy as a straight assertion that music is a language.

The 'literary' aspect of music is to be found, to a greater or less extent, in most Western music written between 1400 and the present day, since music is, properly speaking, a language of the emotions, akin to speech. The appeal of this music is directly to the emotions and, to be fully appreciated, should be responded to in this way.

What he calls the 'literary' type of music he distinguishes from, on the one hand, imitative music which uses motifs taken from bird song or other 'natural' sounds to establish its reference, and more formal or architectural types of music on the other; the latter is exemplified by the *Forty-Eight* or the *Goldberg Variations*.

Both 'literary' and 'architectural' music use the same intervals, progressions and motifs and these have a constant emotional force according to the extended glossary which forms the middle section of his book. This being so, a phrase in a Bach fugue ought not necessarily to express something different from the same phrase in a Beethoven symphony. It seems to me that our musical experience bears this out rather than corroborating Cooke's thesis that two quite different types of musical response are involved. Therefore to save Cooke's thesis from his own reservations I take it as applying quite generally to music of all sorts and periods; he does not argue his case with respect to non-western music, but I do not think there is any reason to suppose that his thesis could not in principle be applied to African or Oriental

music, although presumably there could be differences
in the significance attached to its various elements. As we
have seen, Cooke believes that this language of music is
used to express the emotions of the composer. With
many other supporters of Expressionism he also believes
that music of quality recreates these emotions in the
listener. Cooke's form of Expressionism can be summarised in the following propositions. Music has quality
in so far as:
1 the composer expresses his feelings in it,
2 it accurately reproduces these feelings in the listener.
Note that the music expresses the feeling of the composer; he does not describe his feelings in it, for the
music is an outlet for his feelings just as laughter or tears
may be outlets for emotion: but neither of the latter could
be said to describe one's emotion. We need here to contrast two cases, however. There are occasions when I
may consciously control the expression of my emotions;
I may not give way to them so much as channel their
expression, perhaps in the interests of propriety or perhaps in the interest of influencing other people. Anger
may be none the less real for its being carefully controlled
in order to achieve the maximum effect. On the other
hand, consider cases where we speak of somebody in
paroxysms of grief. Here the grief has taken over to the
extent that the individual is no longer in complete control
of his behaviour. Now it is the former that I suspect
Expressionists have in mind. In the typical case the expression of the emotion is controlled. There may be cases
where a composer has so internalised a musical language as to be able to rush to the keyboard and dash off a
piece without conscious reflection, but these must be
rare.

Possibly the most trenchant critic of Expressionism
was the Viennese music critic Eduard Hanslick, (the critic
pilloried by Wagner as Beckmesser in *Die Meistersinger*;
indeed in an early draft, performed in the presence of
Hanslick, the character was given the name Hans Lich).
Essentially Hanslick's criticism depends upon an assem-
bling of counterexamples.

Firstly, there is music which seems to be notable for the absence of feeling. He cites Bach's *Forty-Eight Preludes and Fugues* as an example of such music. This is a slightly puzzling criticism. Certainly we can ascribe the sorts of 'mental' words we customarily ascribe to works of art to the *Forty-Eight*. We can say of the C sharp minor fugue that it is grave; the music is not as overtly emotional as that of Tchaikovsky, of course, but it would be wrong to say that the words that ascribe mental characteristics to people and which are also used meta- phorically to characterise art cannot be used at all to describe the *Forty-Eight*.

A second criticism is more persuasive. He points out that on the Expressionist thesis we would expect that if two listeners agree on the quality they would agree on the expressive characteristics of the music. If a piece of music is good and is also sad then the two listeners who agree that it is good would feel the sadness themselves and agree in attributing sadness to the composer at the point of composition. But one of the surprising things about music is that listeners at various times have agreed about its quality, but disagreed quite strikingly about its characteristics. Mozart's music seemed tempestuous to its contemporaries but seemed the essence of restraint to later generations. Yet its stature was never in question. Although Hanslick's argument is telling, it does depend upon the premise that there is a degree of variation in the way competent listeners characterise music and this Hanslick surely exaggerates. More worrying for the Expressionist is the fact that the same music can be used in different contexts to express emotions which appear to be mutually incompatible. Hanslick points out that some of the sacred music in the *Messiah* originated in duets by Handel in which it illustrates erotic yearnings.

The English writer, Edmund Gurney[6] a generation later than Hanslick, echoes many of his strictures, pointing out in addition that it is not necessary for the music to recreate feelings in the listener for it to have the char- acteristics it has. We can recognise the music to be sad or gay without feeling sadness or gaiety ourselves. I think this is common experience. It is more frequently the case that we choose music to underscore our moods than that the music determines how we feel.

We can refine the thesis to meet this objection as follows. Under standard conditions (the listener is experienced, co-operative, receptive and prepared to concentrate on the music), the music will infect the listener with its own character. Where it is sad, he will be sad.[7] The thesis is thus now a consciously causal one and it faces a double problem. First we have to find a non-circular account of standard conditions, namely one which makes no reference, explicit or implicit, to how the listener feels when the music is sad. I shall not pursue this particular quest because I think the third criticism above stands. Even if I settle down to listen with no distractions to music by, say, a minor composer of the nineteenth century, I can recognise the music as being sad without feeling sad myself. I do not wish to deny that sometimes a composer wears his heart on his sleeve or that we may not be influenced by the character of the music. This does sometimes happen. All I deny is that these are necessarily connected with the expressive character of the music. As Cooke himself recognises, serene music, for example, may be composed in times of stress; he cites Mozart's *Jupiter*; the sublime *Divertimento K.563* is another example; and we know that Mendelssohn's sunny *Italian Symphony* occasioned him a good deal of sweat. Cooke therefore makes a distinction between the surface feelings and the deeper permanent emotions of the composer which his music expresses.

When we state that a composer, writing a lengthy piece over a long period, expresses his emotions in it, we really ought not to have to explain that we mean his deep, permanent, significant emotions, not the superficial fleeting ones called forth by trivial pleasures and disappointments.

This does look very much like an *ad hoc* device to prevent this rather passé thesis from being falsified. We might briefly observe, too, that this account would make the emotional life of many composers alarmingly unstable, though admittedly only at the deeper level, for many composers engage simultaneously on the production of both tragic and light-hearted works. Brahms, for example, was planning his buoyant *Second Symphony* before the tragic and monumental *First* was completed. Cooke has subsequently stated that he regards the composer as expressing subconscious or even unconscious emotions. But this moves the burden of his theory to an area where neither he nor his critics can offer any evidence. It is probably more realistic to suppose that the emotions of the composer are only contingently connected with his work. The autobiographical evidence seems to confirm this. Thus Berlioz says of the song 'Elegie' which ends his song-cycle *Irlande*, that 'this was the sole occasion on which I was able to express a feeling of the sort directly in music while still under its active influence'. Mozart said that he never felt the emotions attributable to the work when writing music. Mahler, on the other hand, claimed to feel the moods supposed to characterise his music, whereas Tchaikovski, perhaps surprisingly, did not. Neither Hanslick nor Gurney mention one further argument against Cooke's thesis; it is that the predicates we think appropriate descriptions of a piece of music may depend somewhat on the performance. The finale of Beethoven's *Seventh Symphony* may be properly described as tumultuous or Dionysian when played by Toscanini or Solti, but not as played by Klemperer. Yet we might consider both perfectly valid ways of approaching the work. But if the predicates applicable can differ in this way then which of the two, 'tumultuous' or 'massive' (which I take to be incompatible), describes the 'deep unconscious emotions' of the composer?

The conclusion that Hanslick and Gurney draw is that when we describe music as sad or joyful we do so not because we are sad or joyful or because the composer was sad or joyful at the time of composing. It is the music itself which is sad or joyful, witty or sombre. Thus the only alternative that remains is for us to conclude that in the first instance such terms apply to the music itself. 'It is aesthetically quite correct to speak of a theme as having a sad or noble accent but not as expressing the sad or noble feelings of the composer.' The same point has been made recently by R.W. Hepburn. 'I think the stronger *prima facie* case can be made out for the account which claims that emotional qualities can be described, with perfect propriety, as *in* the works of art.' Now there remain, of course, considerable problems as to how we apply these 'mental' predicates to music, what they mean, and how we justify their application. So far we have passed without comment the claim that it is the emotions of the listener which the music arouses, and that it is the emotions of the composer which are being expressed. But is this so? Setting aside the criticisms reviewed above which, in my opinion, render Expressionism untenable, are the mental epithets which are used to describe the character of the music, words which, in their normal context, ascribe emotions to people?

A brief look at some of the psychological research into the reactions of listeners to music may at least make us hesitate, though since students of psychology may not be visited by the niceties which are the professional interest of philosophers, the significance of this work ought not to be overestimated. It might be more interesting to look at the epithets used by critics to describe music. Here are some: expressive, dramatic, bold, unsubtle, effortless, heart-rending, inward, meditative, airy, spontaneous, witty, trance-like, Olympian, dark and brooding, impassioned, dynamic.

Now there are obvious difficulties in describing music, but even bearing in mind the inevitable inexactitude, there is no doubt that most of these epithets do not ascribe emotions where they are used in non-musical contexts. To say that somebody is dynamic or witty is not to ascribe an emotion to him.

There are other more pressing reasons for disputing the thesis that those terms we apply to music ascribe emotions in standard contexts. Emotions have objects; the existence of the object may be an intentional affair in the same sense of intentional as we use to qualify the object of a pictorial representation. They may or may not exist. If I am afraid, then there is something of which I am afraid. My emotions must have an object. Of course I may be afraid of something which does not exist as, for example, children may be afraid of the bogeyman. I may indeed love a non-existent something or somebody. A child may love Santa Claus. Now if music is expressive of emotion then what is the object of that emotion? We have already considered telling objections to the thesis that the emotion is primarily the emotion of the composer or of the listener. If the music expresses the emotion of joy, then who is joyful at what?

The fact is, I believe, that the composer's relation to whatever emotions his music expresses is no closer than the actor's to the characters he portrays: both have a repertoire of devices they exploit. The composer knows what musical devices are expressive of sadness, and if he is commissioned to write a funeral march he calls upon his technique to do so. In the same way the actor who plays Macbeth does not fear the dagger himself but he knows how to represent a man in paraxoysms of fear, and does so. It is no fairer a charge to accuse the composer of insincerity if he writes a successful funeral march for a public figure whom he neither knew nor cared about than it would be to complain if the actor was not really afraid. Sincerity is a much overrated virtue in the arts. It is clear that whenever we characterise music as sad or happy, or ascribe any other of the properties that writers about music borrow from descriptions of the human personality, we speak metaphorically. In raising problems about the possible objects of the emotions music expresses, we have merely shifted the problem. The description of the character of music in terms drawn from the ascription of emotions may be metaphorical but all the other words we listed are equally so. The only advantage in eschewing talk of a language of emotions may be that since emotions have objects there is a further aspect of their metaphorical application to music which we need to justify, namely the identifying of objects of emotion. Words like 'meditative', 'sad' or 'brooding' more commonly ascribe moods than emotions and if, *per impossibile*, we were to attempt a resurrection of the Expressionist thesis, it would be that music is a language of the moods and not a language of the emotions.

Be that as it may, one problem remains to be discussed before we can return to a more general discussion of expressionism. How can we justify the metaphorical application of these expressive predicates to music? Wittgenstein once remarked 'with some people, me especially, the expression of emotion in music, say, is a certain gesture'; many other writers have commented on the connection between music and gesture. But to make something of this clue I think we need to generalise it. Other aspects of behaviour as well as gesture may be revealing of a person's mental state. I shall use 'manner' as the most suitable generic term to cover both behaviour which is intended to convey the individual's mood and attitude and behaviour which 'gives away' his real feelings. We sometimes say of a person that it was not so much what he said as the way he said it (that merited praise or, more often, censure) or, of a person speaking in a language which we do not understand, 'I did not understand what he said but his manner of saying it spoke volumes'. We also sometimes describe somebody as doing a charitable act in an uncharitable manner, for example, somebody who gives to charity but does so begrudgingly.

I suggest that music says nothing, but that the manner of saying nothing speaks volumes. A little less brusquely, we know that gibberish or an unknown tongue may convey no literal meaning to its hearers and yet may convey very forcibly the temper, intentions or reactions of the speaker. The composer Janacek once observed that intonation told him so much he did not need to understand the words. Small children sometimes utter a string of sounds which have no meaning in any known language but which may show that the child is angry or wants something. A scrutiny of those epithets which we apply to music will show that in most cases they ascribe characteristics to the manner of persons. Persons are

witty, brooding, spontaneous; their manner may be heart-
rending, Olympian or even airy. Sometimes such epithets ascribe moods, sometimes not. In my view we can
best explain the function of epithets applied to music by
concluding that they describe the manner of that music.

Since we may apply predicates of manner to persons
or to gibberish, it does not follow from the fact that
similar predicates can be applied to music that music is a
language. Indeed it is easy to see that the expressive
power of music may be a product of its manner without
there being any corresponding language of music. Why
then is the idea that music is a language so ubiquitous?
Perhaps the most obvious way in which music may sustain the linguistic analogy is in the contour of the melodic
line. If a theme is energetic then we expect it to involve
wide intervals, perhaps even to leap from octave to
octave and to be played *mezzo-forte* or *forte.* Similarly, a
person displaying energy moves rapidly in perhaps a
slightly jerky way: slow, languorous movements do not
characterise the energetic man or energetic music.
Somebody whose mood is fiery will express himself in
dramatic and perhaps unexpected gestures, just as the
movement of fiery music is so characterised; on the other
hand, the manner of a person who is sad is restrained and
he will express his sadness sometimes by downward
gestures. In the same way, as Cooke points out, sad
music has restricted melodic intervals and downward
turning melodic lines.

As an example, consider the first movement of
Brahms' violin concerto. The great musicologist and
critic Donald Tovey describes variously the thematic
material of the opening: one theme, which consists of
wide, melodic leaps and is rhythmically rather jerky, is
described as 'energetic': a sinuous and chromatic theme
is described as 'mysterious' whilst the violin's entry with
an upward rushing figure marked forte is described as
'fiery'. All these are predicates of 'manner'.

Other ways of characterising mood in music are by
means of dynamics and timbre. Sad music is normally
quiet; the rich orchestral pallette used, for example, by

Stravinsky in the *Firebird* might not be the most suitable for scoring sad music. Again rhythm and harmony are at the composer's disposal. Slow, steady pulses are conventionally associated with funeral music in western countries, and Cooke has much to say about the associations of minor versus major harmonic progressions. A more complete account is to be found in the glossary which forms a substantial part of his *The Language of Music*. We do not have to subscribe to his Expressionism to recognise the value of this research. Perhaps, too, we ought to stress that the account presumes that gesture and manner are conventional ways of expressing moods and that a culture which shared none of these with us might find it hard to understand the correlations of music and manner which Europeans understand.

Although we can justify the metaphorical ascription of predicates of manner to music and the other arts, a further problem remains; metaphors appear more to invite than to channel responses. If I say that time is a river or that life is a game, my hearer is invited to look for ways of construing my utterance, to look for similarities and relations which would enable him to make sense of my metaphor. But to say that music is sad or gay does not seem to require the active participation of the hearer in quite the same way. The work has already been done.

I suggest then that, although 'the music is sad' is metaphorical, its metaphorical content is pretty minimal; it is well on its way to becoming a dead metaphor together with such expressions as 'weighing the evidence', 'ploughing exams'; these are expressions which began life as metaphors but which have now lost their metaphorical status. The description of music as sad, dynamic, dispassionate, grave, calm, peaceful, etc., has now just a minimal flavour of metaphor, enough to pose a problem about its basis but not enough to warrant interpretation. When a metaphor thus passes into current usage its metaphorical force may not be immediately lost but it is subject to a gradual diminution until the metaphor is dead and the term has passed by catechresis into the dictionary as having that sense. Unless we

recognise the existence of a continuum of 'metaphori-
calness' we will inevitably have difficulty in reconciling
the fact that music is sad or happy in a fairly categorical
manner and in a way in which listeners can agree with the
fact that there is a case to answer on how we ascribe
'mental' predicates to music.[7]

Expressionism is a general theory about the arts, though
perhaps it is not surprising that it has mainly appealed to
those whose first interest is music, lyrical verse or
painting where there may be a relatively short time span
between the initial experience and the work of art which
is supposed to reflect it. In summarising the criticisms we
have made we can bear these arts in mind.

First, the thesis that in art the emotion of the creator is
communicated by the work of art to his public is untest-
able for the great majority of cases. Most of the art we
encounter was produced by writers, painters and
musicians who are now dead and who left no autobiographical evidence, so that the very possibility of
matching their mental states with ours has now dis-
appeared. The problems of comparing what, in some
sense at least, are private mental states are miniscule by
comparison.

Secondly, the Expressionist thesis that art is particularly expressive of the mental state of its creator
cannot serve as a criterion of art. It could be true of other
artefacts, particularly works of craft, that they express the
emotions of the creator. Imagine a woman embroidering
a sampler in sombre colours because she is in a down-
cast mood or a newly bereaved carpenter choosing
ebony for a firescreen.

Thirdly, as we have seen, biographical evidence
strongly suggests that there is a contingent relationship
between the mood of the creator and the artefact. This
suggests that it is the poem and not the poet, the music
and not the composer which is sad or gay. The creator of
the work of art has at his disposal a repertoire of devices
upon which he can draw to produce a work of art with the
characteristics which he requires.

Now there are some exceptions to the general thesis that the qualities of the art are contingently related to the 'mental' characteristics of the creator at the time of creation. A reference to the expressive intentions of the creator cannot always be eradicated. Guy Sircello instances 'calm' 'impersonal' and 'aloof' as examples of such predicates, though 'ironic', 'satiric' and 'witty' strike me as better examples. If the music of Prokofiev or Stravinsky is witty, then the composers were being witty in writing it. If Byron's *Don Juan* is ironic, then the poet was being ironic when he wrote it. However, for the great majority of predicates of manner, the manner characterises the tale but not necessarily the teller. It is certainly true of music and probably true of the other arts as well, that as our familiarity with the art increases we cease to use these expressive predicates. Music critics are not much interested in characterising a new work as sad or joyful nor is it part of the literary critic's job to describe the manner of new poems which he reviews. He may talk about the transformation of thematic material or the particular rhyme schemes and diction used rather than about the manner. But it would be surprising if critics failed to show some basic competence in ascribing these terms when called upon. It is a precondition of the more recondite skills.

Although I have argued that the words which thus characterise the manner of a work of art are not usually words which ascribe emotions in their normal use, there remains a connection between works of art and human emotions. The connection is, however, the obvious one. We love or sometimes even hate works of art. Perhaps some thinkers have confused this with the quite distinct question as to what a work of art can be said to express. Works of art are rarely, in my experience, expressive of love though partly through their being expressive of joy, sadness, calm or serenity they may cause us to love them.

One of the most difficult tasks which the amateur or professional critic faces is distinguishing first of all the admirable from the lovable, and secondly in being sure of

the grounds for the critical judgement of value. It is a
temptation to conclude that a work has quality because
you are fond of it. The sophisticated critic will be aware
that he sometimes loves a work even though it is not
much good. Now it has been suggested that we can in
such cases distinguish liking a work for its qualities and
liking it for its associations with the implication that the
latter are aesthetically irrelevant. Thus I may hate the
Horst Wessel song for its associations, and love Mahler's
Fourth for other associations (perhaps because it was
heard in romantic circumstances). This thesis is that
although these may cause our love or hate neither of
these are aesthetically relevant grounds for love or hate;
the work itself should be both object and cause of my
attitude towards it.

This in turn relies upon a distinction between objects
and cause which has become a commonplace in contemporary philosophy of mind. What causes me to have
an emotion may not be the same as the object of my
emotion. In some cases, of course, they may be identical;
the charging tiger is both cause and object of my
emotion. But my death, for instance, is something I may
well fear and is therefore the object of my emotion, yet it
cannot be the cause since it has yet to occur. The distinction is not entirely clear as it stands; what causal role in
my fear of the charging tiger is played by the beliefs
which I have acquired in the past for instance, beliefs
which seem on all fours with beliefs about the finality and
painfulness of death which I also acquired in the past. Be
this as it may, the associations which a certain image,
word, or phrase of music has for its public is obviously
part of the ambience in which the creative artist thrives.
Maxwell Davies' *St Thomas Wake*, for example, incorporates the associations which a pre-war foxtrot
involves as part of the calculated artistic effect and if such
means are available to the musician how much more for
the writer or artist whose achievement requires a sen-
sitivity to the beliefs which his readers or his public may
have about the objects of representation. It is, I think,
impossible to defend a distinction between features and

mere association with anything like the precision that this thesis seems to require.

The discussion of Expressionism has at length exited in a group of issues about our reaction to art which requires a fuller consideration, a consideration which it will receive in the discussion of interpretation and of pleasure in art.

5

Metaphors of Interpretation and Interpretation of Metaphors

Even a cursory glance at some samples of literary criticism reveals its enormous variety. Looking through a recent collection of criticism of Milton I noticed a discussion of the origin of the word 'romantic', the dating of some of the early poems, and an explanation of why Satan is such a sympathetic figure (to underline the ambiguity of human vices and virtues), a consideration of the influences on Miltonic diction, a discussion of Milton's intentions (to revive faith in those readers whose Christian commitment has been dulled), a discussion of his attitudes to women, and a taxonomy of rhetorical devices in *Paradise Lost*. Though obviously some of these articles were more interesting than others, none was obviously irrelevant to an understanding of the poetry. Moreover the list could easily be paralleled in criticism of any other major writer. So in restricting our attention in this chapter to literary and artistic interpretation we are concentrating on a species of criticism rather than criticism as a whole; however it is certainly arguable that interpretation and the judgement of relative value are regarded as the principal targets of criticism, and all these other activities are only justified in as much as they improve the critic's aim.

The word 'interpretation' is ambiguous. We speak of the interpretation of a poem by a reader or by a critic, and equally we speak of the interpretation of a role by an actor, or the interpretation of a piece of music by a performer or conductor. The obvious difference between the two is that the first consists of a set of statements, whereas the second consists of a set of actions which present the work to the public. However the two forms are not unconnected. If a conductor was to describe the way a piece should go to a master class then his verbal description might amount to that sort of interpretation of a work which might be given by a critic. One can imagine a director describing to an actor what he wants him to do with the part of Hamlet and in describing his conception of the role he might be doing something very similar to what Wilson Knight or Bradley, Coleridge or Johnson might do when they describe how the play should go.

So the two conceptions of interpretation are closely enough related to warrant their being considered together; and yet they differ. A particularly significant distinction is that the audience relies upon an interpretation in the second sense for its encounter with the work of art. This follows from our reflections in Chapter 2 on the ontological differences between works of art. But a more interesting difference comes to our attention when we consider the modes of interpretation that are open to a director. In Peter Hall's recent production of *A Midsummer Night's Dream* the parts of Titania and Oberon and of Theseus and Hypolita were played by the same actors. This doubling of parts is a way of reminding the audience of the symmetry in the play. The fairy king and queen mirror the Duke of Athens and his consort. A rather similar device was used in a recent film of *Hamlet* where a single actress played both Ophelia and Gertrude, a ploy which rather crudely underlines Hamlet's supposedly Oedipal relations with his mother. Now we might reasonably feel that this is not a legitimate way of making critical points. The text offers no licence for doubling, and such an interpretation is the sort that properly belongs to a critical essay. In these circumstances the performance is in part a Midrashic commentary on the play. Nothing more effectively brings out the greater sense of responsibility that musicians currently feel towards their texts than to compare what are regarded as allowable performances in the theatre and in the concert hall. Hans Keller's functional analyses also rearrange the musical text, but he presents these as ersatz lectures consisting only of examples. The case for producing Shakespeare on an apron-stage, in Elizabethan pronunciation and with Elizabethan gesture and performing conventions is quite as strong as the case for original instruments and performing practices in music. In each case the audience will eventually get used to it and will probably be rewarded with a deeper experience of the work.

In either sense of interpretation we judge an interpretation by holding it against the text. We judge an interpretation of *Hamlet* by seeing how it does justice to the text, amongst other things. Equally we judge an interpretation of a Beethoven symphony by considering the performance against the text with its markings, tempo indications and part writing. It is a common complaint that the composer marks his movement *allegro vivace* and the conductor takes it at a *presto*. Now it is important that both interpretation and work be available. A fair interpretation of *Hamlet* presents simultaneously the text and the director or actor's conception. In music a conductor presents both the notes and his conception of the work. But an interpretation which dissects the text in the course of a performance either by alterations to the *dramatis personae* or by cuts, rescoring, or by actually altering the notes or phrasing marked by the composer destroys that delicate balance on which the performing arts depend. The audience expects to read the interpretation in the light of the work which is simultaneously presented. If the latter is distorted to make interpretative points then the entire structure of a performance is undermined. Had they wanted a lecture, they would have gone to one. If they are advised to bring a text of *Hamlet* with them, they know what to expect and what to avoid. If a reasonable justification of the approach which is concerned with 'authenticity' to the text exists it is not to be found in the idea that these works are the deliverances of a demi-god. It is rather that it is very difficult to think oneself into the style of another musician or dramatist so as to make alterations or cuts that actually improve. The least unsuccessful completions, and this is about all that can be claimed on their behalf, are those by pupils or close friends of the creator, such as Sussmayr's completion of Mozart's *Requiem* and Serly's completion of the Bartók *Viola Concerto*. Furthermore, what an author incorporates in his text depends on how he expects the interpreter to perform. The relation is reciprocal: Shakespeare would not have chosen to set the scene in his text if he thought that the scene would be provided by the producer, nor Bach have chosen the instruments and notational devices he did had he not expectations about both timbre and performing conventions. Authenticity thus restores the balance between text and interpretations and still leaves room for the individual artistry of the interpreter. A more subtle producer would have found other ways to make an Oedipal point about Hamlet.[1]

INTERPRETING[1]

Margolis[2] observes that whereas 'description' presumes a publically observable object, disputes over which can be settled by inspection, 'interpretation' implies both an openness towards rival suggestions and a touch of virtuosity. It is quite obvious that much of what a critic does does not count as interpretation. Noting a rhyme scheme, counting the number of a feet in a line, or recognising that a movement is in sonata form count as descriptions rather than interpretations. One reason why we would not regard these as interpretations relates to Margolis' observations; those descriptions require little intelligence or imagination of the reader or listener. To a large extent they are determined by learned criteria. Much the same goes for the ability to recognise transformations of material; that a theme in the third movement is an inversion of one in the first does not require a great deal of musical sensibility, though much more may be required to pick out a more esoteric transformation. A judgement that a novel is about a certain theme, however, seems more a matter of interpretation than simply the giving of a synopsis of the plot. To identify a particular inexplicitly mentioned theme as the underlying subject of a book, or to identify the climax or centre point of a work are unquestionably matters requiring the exercise of taste and judgement and they are paradigmatically those situations where the art of interpretation is exemplified. The more complex and difficult a work is the more it is a case for interpretation. A corollary which I draw from this is much more controversial, and many contemporary thinkers will be found to disagree with it. I believe that interpretations are underdetermined by the work; the work does not itself provide a basis for deciding between two or more plausible and convincing interpretations though it may, of course, provide the basis for dismissing the factitious. Toscanini and Klemperer differ markedly in their views of the *Eroica* as do Jan Kott and Wilson Knight in their approaches to *Hamlet*. But we would be uneasy if we were to dismiss rivals on the grounds that there can be only one 'correct' interpretation. Interpretations begin where the facts end.

If this picture of interpretation is accurate, it seems to rule out the identification of the correct or valid interpretation with what the creator intended. This latter theory has had some distinguished advocates recently: Richard Wollheim, in his Leslie Stephen lecture, 'The Sheep and the Ceremony'[3] endorses it, but it is perhaps most closely associated with E.D. Hirsch.[4] The question as to what interpretation is correct now has an answer; it may not however be a single answer. The creator may have intended that the work be ambiguous between several different specific interpretations but the totality of these comprise the correct answer to our question. Of course such intentionalism excludes, for performing arts as well, the openness to interpretation which I have stressed.

What, then, does Hirsch have to say about the fact that critical interpretations vary? He answers that such alternatives remain at best only partial views. Now in part Hirsch's work is a reaction against the anti-intentionalism which marked post-war writing on the theory of literary criticism both amongst critics and philosophers. So this is perhaps an appropriate point to review that debate before we return to the problems raised by the diversity of interpretation.

INTENTIONS

'Celfydd celed ei arfaeth' (Let art hide its causes). One of the most celebrated of modern controversies in aesthetics centres on the use critics ought to make of information about the intentions of the author. Since the war, the anti-intentionalist faction has had the upper hand, very largely because of the profound influence it has had amongst literary critics. The following quotation from a famous article by W.K. Wimsatt and M.C. Beardsley[5] crystallises their position: 'The design or intention of the author is neither available nor desirable as a standard for judging the success of a work of art.' This is not, of course, altogether a judgement about what critics do for there can hardly be much doubt that they do frequently cite authorial intention; sometimes they may take into account what a writer says about his purposes in order to get a lead on weaknesses, whether real or apparent. It is simply false to say that the design or intention of the author is not available; sometimes it is and where it is not, we may wish that it were. No critic in his right mind will ignore Lawrence's letter to Garnett in which he said of *The Rainbow*, 'You mustn't look in my novel for the old stable ego character', and no reader will doubt that it expresses Lawrence's conception of his work. What is undeniable, of course, is that such knowledge cannot directly affect our judgement of the merit of the work; it is what it is, good, bad, or indifferent, irrespective of the status the author intended it to have. The history of art is littered with failed masterpieces, and the intentions of their creators cannot help them a jot. On occasion, a work may even be better than intended; thus Louis Armstrong maintained to the end that he was just an entertainer, though many of his admirers rate him far more highly. However there may be a more indirect connection between our knowledge of the author's intentions either before he created the work or during its creation, and our evaluation of the finished product. For if authorial hints on how we should interpret it become available, then by taking these into account we may understand the work better. This is by no means a necessary truth: the author can have a distorted view of the significance of his work and it may also be very different from what he intended. Of course, writers are sometimes articulate about their aims. Henry James, for example, was an extremely conscious artist who sought to control quite strictly the effects in his work, but it is not inconceivable that he was unaware of the sexual significance of that scene in *The Turn of the Screw* where the governess watches, fascinated, as little Flora is 'markedly and intently trying to tighten in its place' a fragment of wood in a flat piece which contains a hole. (We do not have to imagine that the title of the story has any erotic significance.) If then we broaden our conception of the intention of the author so as to embrace both conscious and unconscious intentions then it does seem perverse to deny that knowledge of these, which could come from letters, conversations and other sources outside the work, may help us to understand the work.

Now most philosophers, critics and readers would agree that understanding is an essential precondition of evaluation. There is then an indirect relation between the two. Admittedly, we might have reservations about a work which became more interesting once we took into account certain biographical knowledge; we may well think that a greater achievement would be a work which stood on its own two feet and whose interpretation relied simply on the understanding of ideas and beliefs current at the time of writing. Such a work would be, in the critical jargon, more 'fully achieved'. It is also worth observing that the knowledge which we have of what an author was attempting during writing is usually more interesting than the plans which he has before he started, for the latter are mutable. In either case such information may tell us what to look for in a work. Hardy described *Jude the Obscure* as 'a miserable achievement compared with what I intended'. Although the remark is by no means specific, it may still give us a lead to what we should look out for in reading the novel. More useful still might be the information from a letter that Conrad wanted to alter *The*

Secret Agent in proof but was deterred by the cost.

A preoccupation with intentions may be misconceived for very different reasons. Creative writers, musicians or artists will sometimes describe how the work may take over so that their choices are circumscribed by the decisions they have already made. The work of art begins to take on a life of its own and it is as though the subsequent properties it has are inevitable granted its beginning. I believe this is connected with the unity and coherence which many of the greatest works display. It is illustrated in a remarkable observation Pushkin makes in a letter: 'Do you know that that Tatyana of mine has shown Eugene the door. I simply would not have believed her capable of such a thing.' The fact that the work may, as a consequence, develop characteristics very different from those envisaged by the creator before he started work shows that evidence as to the author's intentions needs to be weighed against the work; it cannot be taken at face value. Though words are the medium of writers, they may deceive themselves about the character of a work, they may deliberately mislead others from pique or irritation, and they may quite easily have forgotten what they intended. If statements by writers about their intentions can be so unreliable, how much more care must we take with the reports of artists and musicians for whom words may not be the natural mode of expression, and whose self-descriptions may consequently be profoundly misleading.

Beardsley[6] argues that many references to intentions in criticism are eliminable. They are merely misleading ways of talking about the work itself. Thus Cleanth Brooks says that in the fourth stanza of the *Immortality Ode*, the strained effect is intentional, and then remarks in a footnote that whatever Wordsworth intended, the strained effect fits. Now it may well be that many critical remarks can be rephrased in this way without much loss, though we should not hastily conclude that the original expression and its paraphrase have the same meaning. On the other hand many critical observations which refer to the attitudes or intentions of the author cannot so easily be eliminated. Shakespeare's *Henry V* has been much debated because the king, superficially the acme of kingly virtue, demonstrates a sadistic streak more proper to the representation of a psychopath. Derek Traversi says of this:

It would be wrong to suppose that Shakespeare, in portraying Henry, intends to stress a note of hypocrisy. His purpose is rather to bring out certain contradictions, human and moral, which seem to be inherent in the notion of a successful king.[7]

On the surface, it looks as though Beardsley might simply replace this by the assertion that Henry (the dramatic character) is not a hypocrite, but is prey to certain contradictory impulses through his position as a successful monarch. However we lose the reference to the authorial intention at our peril, for we view the play differently if we think that Shakespeare was not criticising the king. The dangers are much clearer in the case of irony or satire. If we distinguish what is said in the poem, play or fiction from what the author meant by it, then irony can be defined in terms of such a gap between the sentence-meaning of the lines and utterer's meaning. Beardsley's own example is now very familiar; it concerns Housman's couplet

> Get you the sons your fathers got
> And God will save the Queen.

from his jubilee poem, *1887.* Frank Harris apparently congratulated Housman on his irony, much to the author's annoyance. (There is some evidence that Housman was being disingenuous when he claimed that the poem was intended seriously.) If the poem is indeed ironic then what the words mean and what Housman meant by them diverge. At face they are an instruction to fathers to produce sons to fight for the Queen; if the lines are ironic then Housman registers disgust at a society which expects its children to lay down their lives for an élite of pampered and privileged nonentities who only hold the position they do through the accident of birth.

It is certainly possible for a reader to take an ironic poem at face value. Often it can be very difficult, if not impossible, to discover whether the author's intention was ironic or not: Marvell's *Horatian Ode* is hard to construe for this very reason. These are paradigmatically the cases where evidence outside the text may be crucial. Beardsley's claim that irony must be found in the poem itself and that a poem is ironical if the irony is found there by competent critics glosses over the difficulty. Critics might quite possibly agree that a poem is ironic when the author was not being ironic, or vice versa. The knowledge that a writer is consistently ironical may be based on evidence external to the work, evidence which is relevant and crucial in establishing whether a text is or is not ironical. Such evidence, of course, we need to weigh against the text to see whether a reading that reverses the apparent sense is possible; that much we can concede to Beardsley. But even if we agreed with him that the text provides all that is relevant in determining the meaning, the very characterising of it is as ironic implies an authorial stance, an implication which Beardsley cannot gainsay. If a text is ironic then the author intended to be ironic when he wrote it. What seems to elude Beardsley is that every such judgement about the text entails a parallel judgement about the tone and manner of the writer. These references to Intentions are not eliminable.

If Beardsley is prepared to allow the possibility that critical statements about the intention of the author are relevant only if they can be derived from the statements the text contains, then the fact that irony may quite properly be gauged from extra-textual considerations shows that critics depart from his prescriptions. If he allows no claims about authorial stance at all then he excludes irony from the repertoire of critical concepts with quite devastating results for the practice of criticism. (I pass over the difficulties in deducing an ironical tone from the text alone.)

His treatment of the performing arts is equally open to objection. Here he argues that references to the composer's intentions are eliminable in favour of statements about what sounds better in the context. There are many examples of a composer scoring his music in such a way that apparently important inner parts are inaudible or where technical improvements in the instrument invite revision. The coda of the first movement of Schubert's great *C Major Symphony* contains a miscalculation, so that a woodwind theme is inaudible. Some conductors give the theme to the trumpets. Tovey advocates using Schubert's unrevised scoring of the string parts. A celebrated case of the second category is the scoring in Beethoven's *Fifth Symphony* where a phrase is given first to the horns and then to the bassoons. Now since at that time the horns, lacking valves, could not have played the second passage, it has become accepted practice to rescore it for the horns which now, equipped with valves, can play it without difficulty. Finally, there is a passage in the scherzo of Beethoven's *Ninth* where the strings cover the woodwind. Like the Schubert example, this looks like a miscalculation but here we have no alternative version to help out. In both cases we assume that the composer intended a part to be heard and rescore to help him out. In the second case, we are on stickier ground because it might well be argued that Beethoven, knowing that horns could not play the theme on its second occurrence, took that into account in his calculation of the texture.

None of these quite fits Beardsley's account; we are not simply deciding what sounds better. In any case what sounds better is relative to individual taste and to the taste of the time. We may learn to appreciate Bach on original instruments without thinking it sounds better at first hearing. We persevere because we think that the sounds of eighteenth-century instruments were in Bach's mind when he composed, and that the sounds he intended ought to be recovered. Beardsley himself acknowledges the importance of recovering the original sound: but then it is no longer a matter of doing what sounds better, but rather of trying to reconstruct the original practice in matters of ornamentation, tempi, *notes inégales*, size of forces and phrasing. Some might admire those earlier generations of interpreters who pulled around the tempi and phrasing and used lavish *portamenti* (scooping), justifying it on the grounds that it sounded better that way, but such a high-handed approach now seems to most of us self-indulgent and egotistical.

There are limits. The deficiencies of the natural trumpet and horn meant that some notes in the scale were out of tune, a fact lamented by eighteenth-century writers. The critic Runciman, writing in the 1840s, argued that the sound of basses not quite in tune was essential to the effect of mysteriousness in Beethoven and that the better ensemble of his time dispelled that effect. I doubt whether we would wish to recapture either of these effects.

In other respects the situation is similar to that which obtains with respect to literature. The composer's *obiter dicta*, his letters, his gramophone recordings and the interpretative tradition may all help us in performing a work. They may give us some guide to his intentions at the time the work was written, or they may suggest that his ideas changed subsequently. But they are not infallible and they are not part of the text. There is an interpretative tradition that the trumpet part at one point in Elgar's *Second Symphony* should be prolonged because in the first performance the player played it so; Elgar liked the effect and it became part of the tradition. He certainly did not intend it at the time of composing, the notation is clear about that, and he did not change the text in accordance with his second thoughts. Interpreters therefore make up their own mind about the matter. Stravinsky's famous remarks about Karajan's interpretation of the *Rite of Spring* (*'tempo di hoochie-coochie'*) and his castigation of Boulez for excessive speed did not necessarily indicate his intentions. A half a century had elapsed since composition. His preference in matters of tempo is just one amongst many possible views and in fact his own tempi are faster than those of Boulez. However to make the point against Beardsley, all that is required is the recognition that sometimes evidence of the composer's intentions may exist independently of the score. Then it would be both doctrinaire and contrary to musical practice to ignore it.

Indeed, to a great extent the two attitudes towards the relation of intention and work reflect the difference between the enclosed and open conception of a work of art. The reader, listener or viewer for whom a work of art is essentially a created object which may reflect both culture and creator is the man for whom intentions are not irrelevant. The reader, listener or viewer for whom the work is simply an aesthetic object akin to a naturally occurring object or scene will prefer an anti-intentionalist approach. For the latter Webern's dictum holds: 'Between the products of nature and those of art no essential difference prevails.' I take the former view because, as I have already suggested, created objects form a sub-class of the objects of aesthetic interest, namely those which are objects for interpretation. It is in virtue of this that they possess aesthetically important structural features. So there is a general sense in which intentions are relevant in that, since works of art are artefacts, they must be the product of an intended act of creation. In this somewhat minimal sense, intention is a condition of something counting as art. We will not take the same attitude to a 'poem' printed out by a computer as we do to one by Ted Hughes.

The fundamental misconception to which we are all, from time to time, prey, is to see the critic's interpretative comments as a surrogate for what the author could have said had he the mind to. In the case of living authors the nagging suspicion remains that at any time he or she may descend with the magisterial 'This is what I meant'. If the point of *Princess Casamassima* is that Hyacinth's consciousness is selective, why did not Henry James say so and thereby spare critics and public a great deal of time.

The reaction against the movement led by Beardsley and Wimsatt has not everywhere taken the form of the arguments I have presented and which, I believe, make a case for a weaker form of anti-intentionalism. Instead, as I have mentioned, E.D. Hirsch, in his spirited and influential *Validity in Interpretation*, has argued that the criterion of correctness in interpretation is to be found in the the meaning of the author. The meaning of a text is thus to be identified with what the author intended it to mean. Hirsch dismisses the idea that interpretations are correct relative to the world-view of the interpreter; the meaning of a text does not change; the task of criticism is the 're-cognition' of the author's meaning through the text. On the fact of it such a thesis is extremely restrictive. What about those implications which the author might not have considered? What about Freudian slips? Hirsch however operates with a sufficiently relaxed conception of intention to allow unconscious or unintended meanings provided they 'fall within the whole' of the meaning. He does not rule out cases such as a computer printed poem having a meaning. Since he collapses the idea of sentence-meaning (what a string of words means according to the grammar and semantics of the language) and utterer's meaning (what the speaker or writer meant by them), a string of words cannot have a meaning unless somebody intends them to have that meaning. But by using an expansive conception of intention, the practical consequences of his approach may not prove so different from those of Beardsley who recommends that we attend to the sentence-meaning and treat the utterer's meaning as inaccessible save in so far as the sentence-meaning reveals it.

Hirsch's use of the term 'interpretation' is not altogether consistent. Sometimes he speaks as though interpretation is simply the understanding of the text in the sense of understanding the sentences it contains in the most minimal way. In this sense any reading of anything involves interpretation; the reader of a popular newspaper interprets the few short sentences it contains in lieu of news. But Hirsch also uses it in its more common and more specialised sense of eliciting themes in a work, contrasting that with understanding the meaning of the words at their most basic level.

I do not think it is accidental that writers who believe that the meaning of a text is to be identified with authorial intentions are also those who appear to have the model of the physical sciences at the back of their minds. This is quite explicit in the work of Hirsch, who treats an interpretation as a falsifiable hypothesis about the authorial meaning which is made probable by the evidence. It is also, I think, present in the recent book by Frank Kermode, *The Genesis of Secrecy*, which treats interpretation as the uncovering of latent elements in the text which are often intentionally concealed by the author. On occasion this is because the author wishes to restrict access to the truths to the dedicated and spiritually-minded reader; this may have been true of the Gospel writers, and may also have been true of Milton. On other occasions, the authors may tease the public; Joyce remarked: 'I've put in so many enigmas and puzzles that it will keep the professors busy for centuries over what I meant, and that's the only way of ensuring one's immortality.' The assumption again is that there is an answer to the question what the text means and it lies in what the author intended to mean by it. The task of the critic then is to determine what the author meant, and this requires a methodology akin to that of the scientist: in each case hypotheses are pondered, and accepted or dismissed on the basis of whatever evidence is currently or becomes available. But Hirsch does not show that it is proper to speak of interpretations as being correct. If 'This interpretation is probably true' makes sense, then 'This interpretation is true' makes sense. But both these formulations seem to do violence to the way we commonly speak about interpretations. Interpretations are multifarious and they are underdetermined by the work in question.

We can exemplify this point by considering the way in which interpretations in another art, music, are widely recognised as dividing into two categories. There are interpretations which preserve a classical balance and lucidity, which deliberately set out to reproduce the intentions of the composer faithfully in so far as the score represents these, and which strive for objectivity. These I shall call Apollinian. Interpreters who represent this particular strain are, most evidently, conductors like Klemperer, Haitink, Weingartner and, perhaps, Karajan.

As an example of the second, Dionysian, sort of conductor we might turn to Furtwangler who strikes me as
representing the Dionysian virtues *par excellence*. For
Furtwangler, the score was a starting point from which,
by subtle changes of tempi and certain ways of handling
the ensemble he could, at his finest, produce an effect
which struck the hearers as both echt-Furtwangler and
yet as perfectly in keeping with the spirit of the music.
Nietzsche's distinction thus crudely appropriated might
seem to demand that we divide musicians exclusively
into the two classes; nothing could be further from the
truth, of course. Toscanini seemed to incorporate both
elements, as did Beecham, despite the liberties he took
with the composer's directions. And if the pianist
Solomon seems a paradigm of the Apollinian approach,
such a conclusion might not survive our hearing his
classic and impassioned reading of the Brahms' Second
Piano Concerto.

This distinction, of course, applies to the performing
arts alone; we would not naturally divide critical studies
offered by, say, Coleridge and Johnson in this way. My
point in introducing the distinction is to show how widely
accepted amongst interpretative artists is the diversity of
those interpretations; it is a fact about their understanding of the art which cannot be lightly set aside. A
musical score, no matter how precise its directions,
cannot totally determine the exact volume of an *mf* or a
pp nor the exact speed of *allegro con brio*. Attempts by
composers like Messiaen at total serialism where even
dynamics are fully notated fall short of completely determining the sound. It is indeed noteworthy that a
composer like Mahler whose scores are littered with extremely minute instructions nevertheless is interpreted
in a wide variety of ways, many of which are very convincing; indeed the diversity of interpretations seems to
be more a feature of the interpretation of Mahler than of
many other composers. Indeed the diversity of interpretations is one mark of greatness in a work.

It is this variability of interpretation which I think rules
out a scientific model of critical understanding; in the

next section I shall exemplify this variety in literary criticism and consider its implications.

THE VARIETY OF INTERPRETATIONS

As we have seen, the variety of interpretations possible for a piece of music is acknowledged. The same holds for literature. The central theme of *Hamlet* was thought by Bradley to be the Prince's melancholy temperament; Ernest Jones argued that the pivot was the Prince's Oedipal relationship with Gertrude and that this accounted for his procrastination. Indeed Hamlet's delay was a preoccupation of the first detailed study of the play by Thomas Hanmer, as well as of many subsequent discussions. An interesting rejoinder to this traditional preoccupation is that of Helen Gardner who maintains that the conventions of revenge tragedy required that the avenger await a suitable opportunity: the genre thus demanded delay; once this is recognized we see that Johnson's criticism that Hamlet 'is rather an instrument than an agent' is wide of the mark. Contemporaries would not have seen the Prince as the victim of events which prevented him from carrying out his task. These delays were familiar aspects of the genre, and not particular faults in a particular play. (Even if this were not the case the Prince's delay can be given a rational explanation in terms of the Elizabethan debate over the existence of ghosts and in particular the discussion as to whether they are 'spirits of health or goblins damned'.) Amongst more recent critics Jan Kott in Cracow in 1956 found it impossible to see the play as other than a poiitical drama; Wilson Knight sees the play as a study of physical and spiritual death; Fergusson views it as a ritual drama. The interpretations of perhaps the most studied of all works of literature are legion.

The existence of such a multitude of accounts provokes the question, do these critics believe that they are making assertions about their own reaction to the play?, about the response of the general theatre-goer?, or about the response of the critically aware? Are they simply making disguised attempts at persuasion? (Look at the play this way, you will find it rewarding!) or are they making claims about the play itself? I will name these different positions the subjective, inter-subjective, persuasive and descriptive, respectively. There are two forms of the inter-subjective thesis; interpretations may represent the response of the critically qualified, or they may represent the response of simply those who have experienced the work in question, regardless of qualifications. The argument against the subjective and inter-subjective accounts of interpretations are very simple and straight-forward but, none the less, conclusive. There is critical disagreement amongst scholars and critics about inter-pretation. Some interpretations are dismissed on the grounds that they are incompatible with the evidence of the text. This riposte has been made to the interpretation of *Hamlet* offered by Wilson Knight: Weitz[8] argues that Knight 'distorts or omits some of the obvious facts of the play'. 'Knight's conception of the Hamlet universe as one of health, strength and humanity, with Hamlet the only sick individual in it, seems utterly perverse and about as far from the 'poet's centre of consciousness' as one could get.' If anything, as Fergusson amongst others points out, it is the other way around. The Hamlet universe, which includes the court, is corrupt, unhealthy, rotten, founded on murder and incest, and Hamlet is the healthy one seeking, not decisively to be sure, to uncover and scourge 'the hidden impostume'. Now such a reply would be beside the point if the interpretation simply reported the experience of Wilson Knight, for the record he offers is then simply autobiographical. The facts at issue would then be merely whether Knight had the experience of the play his interpretation records. He would have had to have experienced the play as contrast-ing the sickness of Hamlet with the normality of Denmark, and what the text said would only be relevant in so far as it indirectly enabled us to form judgements about the experience of this reader. Equally, whether the interpretation is supposed to be either a judgement about the verdict of the public at large, or about the verdict of the critically aware, a similar proviso goes. The relevant facts are not immediately facts about the play, but facts about the public or the critics' peers. So the subjective and both forms of the inter-subjective theory fail on these same grounds: the text is a basis for evaluating interpretations.

The persuasive theory is, unfortunately, question-begging. We recommend a particular interpretation of a play because we think it is valid. So in order to account for the persuasive force behind an interpretation we need have already an account of what it is for an interpretation to be valid and that, of course, is the point at issue.

Although descriptivism seems the least implausible of the various alternatives, the existence of a variety of interpretations seems to pose a difficulty at least in as much as we hesitate to conclude that of two mutually incompatible interpretations, one must be true and the other false. Now although this naturally follows from what we have said about the under-determination of interpretations, we nevertheless need to understand how a critic may allow for rival accounts and it is to this that we now turn.

In a cool hour, critics are willing to admit the possibility of an understanding of a play which differs from their own. When we consider the complexity of works of art and the differing backgrounds which readers bring this is perhaps not surprising. Dr Johnson's words are worth quoting in this connection.

He who differs from us does not always contradict us . . . we have less reasons to be surprised or offended when we find others differ from us in opinion, because we very often differ from ourselves.

. . . as a question becomes more complicated and involved, and extends to a greater number of relations, disagreement of opinion will always be multiplied, not because we are irrational, but because we are finite beings furnished with different kinds of knowledge, exerting different degrees of attention, one discovering consequences which escape another, none taking on the whole concatenation of causes and effects . . . each comparing what he observes with a different criterion, and each referring it to a different purpose (Bate, W.J. *Samuel Johnson*, p.532).

The strength of an intentionalist approach like that of Hirsch lies in the fact that there are constraints on possible interpretations. A famous line in one of Shakespeare's most famous sonnets reads: 'Bare ruin'd choirs where late the sweet birds sang.' If we allow ourselves total licence in forming interpretations there should be no objection to construing the lines in any way we find interesting. According to American prison argot, informers 'sing'; why not take the line as describing a derelict prison? The answer is obvious. The words could not have had this sense in Shakespeare's day. If, however, we argue this way as we frequently do in dismissing more general Marxist and Freudian interpretations which seem to us anachronistic, are we not conceding that the sense we think we can give to this line depends upon what the author intended?

Empsom offers the following gloss on the line:

To take a famous example, there is no pun, double syntax, or dubiety of feeling, in
    'Bare ruin'd choirs, where late the sweet birds sang',
but the comparison holds for many reasons; because ruined monastery choirs are places in which to sing, because they involve sitting in a row, because they are made of wood, are carved into knots and so forth, because they used to be surrounded by a sheltering building crystallised out of the likeness of a forest, and coloured with stained glass and painting like flowers and leaves, because they are now abandoned by all but the grey walls coloured like the skies of winter, because the cold and narcissistic charm suggested by choir-boys suits well with Shakespeare's feeling for the object of the Sonnets, and for various sociological and historical reasons (the Protestant destruction of monasteries; fear of puritanism), which it would be hard now to trace out in their proportions; these reasons, and many more relating the simile to its place in the Sonnet, must all combine to give the line its beauty, and there is a sort of ambiguity in not knowing which of them to hold most clearly in mind. Clearly this is involved in all such richness and heightening of effect, and the machinations of ambi-

136 *Contemporary Aesthetics*

guity are among the very roots of poetry.[9]

Now it is interesting to note that we shall allow these implications of the line which are consonant with the sense that the line would have borne in Elizabethan days even if there is no direct evidence that those were intended by the writer. Indeed even if he had left other directions about its interpretation we would still feel free to interpret it as suggesting a similarity between church and forest. So it seems that the constraints upon interpretations are such as to allow only those that the author, writing at the time he did, *could* have intended. We exclude those he could have intended had he written at a time when the words had other senses and we, of course, exclude interpretations which rely upon giving the words senses which they have never had. The meaning of the text, then, is always a constraint within which we may construct our interpretations. Of course an intentionalist need not insist that the creator consciously formulate the varying significances to be found in his work. To take an example from painting, the point of the cat in Monet's Olympia has been much debated. The painter said that he put it in because he liked cats. He was probably being disingenuous. Even if he was not, we may still take the cat as an obvious erotic symbol, and as a playful reversal of the tradition of showing a lap-dog as a symbol of domesticity. The associations and implications of a word or image form part of the repertoire which any writer or painter masters, and which it is part of his art to employ, and it is not in the least implausible to suppose that he so internalises these as to use them without conscious reflection. This belongs, perhaps, more to the shared beliefs about various objects than strictly to its sense and its sense alone. If, indeed, he possessed idiosyncratic beliefs, we may allow these a part in a permissible interpretation. But beyond this point interpretations become mere idle intellectual games played by critics.

It may well seem that this leaves now too small a place for the authorial intention in determining the interpretation. It would be absurd to pretend that *Hard Times* was anything else than a bitter attack on Victorian industrial society and its education system; it would be equally absurd to deny that Dickens intended it as such and that there is a connection between his intentions in writing the novel and the interpretation which we give it. What room then do we have to choose between rival readings of this novel? Can we see it as an analysis of marriage in Victorian times? There are these elements in the novel, of course, but it would be preposterous to regard them as anything else but peripheral in the light of the novel's overwhelming insistence on the political and social themes. It is also very clear that the novelist himself has a point of view which he does not disguise. It is because of this last fact that we may well regard *Hard Times* as bearing a similarity as much to allegory and satire as to imaginative fiction proper. It resembles *Pilgrim's Progress* or *Gulliver's Travels* as much as it resembles *Portrait of a Lady*. In these works, unlike imaginative fiction, the authorial voice is plain and the scope for interpretation restricted by that fact. These, then, are not works of imaginative art but rather literary productions with many aesthetic merits to beguile the student of literature. We study them for the prose style or for their narrative structure, but we do not, save where they border on imaginative literature, contrast and choose amongst interpretations in the same way. The key to the unlocking of the themes is given to us explicitly or by clear implication. When the advocate of an ideology requires that a work side with one particular party, he is effectively excluding imaginative art. Even here, though, an endorsement of an authorial viewpoint makes space available for the interpretative work to go on. For, as Kermode remarks, what is so easily achieved is merely the starting point for further inquiry. The keys which establish the general character of a satire or a *roman à clef* do not preclude the work of interpretation at a more minute and detailed level. To a large extent the genre defines the precise place and scope of the interpretations.

THE TOPOGRAPHY OF INTERPRETATIONS

If my arguments so far are to the point, the reader will find it puzzling that critics do not advocate their favoured interpretations in quite the take it or leave it way that their own principles suggest they ought. They often speak as though their views are right and as though the interpretations they profer characterise the work itself. This is not easily made compatible with the assumption that a variety of interpretations is possible. If the principles to which many pay lip-service were firmly adhered to then disagreements ought to be less frequent than they really are. The critic is torn between generosity in recognising the possibility of other approaches and the natural desire to press his own. Is there any way of reconciling these two considerations?

A topographical metaphor may help. There is no reason why a critic may not recognise and welcome other approaches whilst advertising his own. He can do this whilst insisting that his own interpretation is a description of the work. Commonly, a critic will propose his own reading as the central or core reading of the work to which others are more or less peripheral. If you regard *Hamlet* as essentially a play about revenge then you may allow that there are other ways of looking at it but place these to the periphery; to enliven a dead metaphor, the others are eccentric. A commitment to one reading places the others in a certain pecking order. Given the view of *Hamlet* as a play about procrastination, the Bradleyan interpretation is comfortably close whilst Ernest Jones' view becomes highly peripheral. Indeed, when an interpretation is highly peripheral on the majority of existing interpretations it is contentious, an odd view to take. It is also obvious that the history of criticism is in large part a history of argument and counter-argument about interpretative claims. This holds whichever sense of interpretation we have in mind for interpretative traditions in criticism and performance interlock. The creator of the role of Shylock was a celebrated clown, Thomas Doggett.[10] Macklin seems to have been the first actor to present Shylock as a serious figure, a malevolent and villainous character. To Kean we owe the tradition of presenting him sympathetically, as a persecuted representative of a persecuted race. Irving intensified this trend by treating him as a tragic hero. There has been considerable debate in this century as to the propriety of this interpretation. Stoll claimed that Shylock was a stock Elizabethan comic villain. For all the arguments we consider in favour of recreating authentically Elizabethan performing practices, it would clearly be morally impossible so to present Shylock in an age which has seen Belsen and Auschwitz, and it is to our credit that we place moral above aesthetic considerations here.

Again, as we have seen, some interpretations are so widely accepted that critical work becomes a matter of investigating the detail. Furthermore some interpretations do not so much relegate others to the fringe of the universe of discourse as rule them out altogether. If *Hamlet* is seen as the agent who will cleanse the rotten state of Denmark then one cannot simultaneously follow Wilson Knight in viewing him as the one abnormal element in a healthy and sane society. This exclusiveness is, of course, much more frequent in the performing arts. An interpreter may think that his is the 'right' way to play Beethoven's *Waldstein*, whilst admitting that there are other viable approaches. But he obviously cannot simultaneously present the work in two quite different ways; to take one interpretative crux, he cannot present the slow movement simultaneously as a mere bridge between two huge movements, a movement to be played swiftly and with the minimum of weight and at the same time present it as a serious and profound movement anticipating the slow movements of the last period, a movement which, despite its brevity, is the focal point of the sonata. The diversity of interpretation is largely peculiar to the arts. A philosophical text is also, of course, an object of interpretation but whereas the critic assumes that his interpretation is not correct in the sense that it is the sole viable reading of the text, the assumption behind philosophical inquiry into, say, Hume's *Treatise*, is that Hume was endeavouring to convey a single picture of human knowledge. Certainly very few scholars would insist that theirs is the only reading the text allows, and in that sense it is perfectly true that the text under-determines the interpretation much as a work of art does. But this is not a state of affairs that either the author or his reader prefers. The attempt is always to determine one particular reading and any community of scholars hopes that one particular account of what Hume was trying to say will take the palm. It is no merit in a philosophical treatise that it sustains many interpretations, even though it is perhaps inevitable, given the ambiguity of language and the very painstaking and gradual progress of philosophy towards greater precision.

Ask a philosopher what he meant and you should get a reply (unless he has forgotten). To put the question to a writer is impertinent and you may get a dusty answer. It is said that when a correspondent asked Tolstoy what *War and Peace* meant, he received the several volumes of the novel complete as a reply. Picasso wisely remained cagey when asked the significance of the horse and bull represented in *Guernica*, refusing to enlarge on the observation that the horse represented the people and the bull unrestrained violence. Even then he might have gone too far. When a variety of interpretations are available then it is one task of the critic to create his own topography of the various approaches that are available; he not only isolates what he deems the central theme, but he places alternative views in the geography of the understanding of the work. Some of these elements may be the products of his own observation, and some the products of other critics. Ideally he should relate them. In a penetrating study of *Nostromo*, Tillyard[11] identifies a tragic theme, the study of ideals and their corruption, a Christian theme, and a world of magic.

Like the railway and Charles Gould, Montero repeats early South American history, but just as surely he is the malicious fairy, slighted, resentful, and bent on mischief, at the christenting feast of the infant railway. Once we see Montero in this guise (and Conrad leaves us here to our own inferences) we find the fairy theme, with its kin the ballad theme all over the place, often explicitly mentioned.

He notes the striking way in which Conrad 'creates the illusion of a world being lived all at once by a great number of very different people'.

'There were a few children, too, more or less naked, crying and clinging to the legs of their elders. He had never before noticed any sign of a child in his patio . . . '
. . . Gould may not have known the existence of these people, but Conrad did, and long before he thought fit to mention them. That mention indeed is a wonderful stroke, quite unexpected and bearing the imprint of absolute truth. These secret hangers-on of the great house are, after an instant's reflection, what we know would exist in a country afflicted by the extremes of poverty and wealth. If Conrad is at home with them (and was any novelist more aware of the refuse of humanity?), so much the more is he likely to be at home with the central areas of human society.

But central to the novel, in his view, is the political theme and it is around this that these other elements may be ranged.

Miss Bradbrook wrote in 1941, 'What else in Conrad has dated, his politics are contemporary'. And again, 'Conrad's political writings are few, but almost without exeption they are apt to the present time'. The general sentiment is as true today as in 1941; Conrad's politics are frighteningly real: but his political writings bulk larger than Miss Bradbrook allows. *Nostromo*, though so much else, is a political novel, and, as such, ampler and of a deeper wisdom than the *Secret Agent* and *Under Western Eyes*.

CRITICAL REASONS AND THE HERMENEUTIC CIRCLE

Some works of art may offer few opportunities for critical interpretation; if, however, my thesis holds for at least most of those works of art which are particularly distinguished, then we can draw certain conclusions about critical reasoning. Critical reasons certainly cannot be probative in the fullest sense. A reason for advocating a certain interpretation of a play cannot establish that interpretation to the exclusion of others. By the same token we cannot assume that these reasons render more probable the interpretation they favour. For the proposition that an interpretation is probable permits the expansion into 'The interpretation is probably true', and there are no grounds for supposing that a sense can be given to 'Bradley's interpretation of Hamlet is probably true'. Any probabilistic judgement presupposes that there is a true judgement which would supplant it were we able to tell what the facts of the situation really are. Although critics and thinkers about art differ on whether the mere existence of a complete work of art entails that 'all the facts are in', or whether knowledge about the author's intentions or other 'background information' is relevant, nevertheless most unite in agreeing that even when 'all the facts are in' (whatever the facts are), interpretations are under-determined. It is central to the concept of a work of art that it may be read or performed in various ways. Contrariwise, if it is probably the case that Mars supports microscopic life then it is, as a matter of fact, either true or false. We can in this, if not in every, case imagine that further tests would settle the question. But we could hardly imagine that more information would settle the question as to whether *Nostromo* is primarily a political novel or not, or whether Hamlet's relationship with Gertrude is Oedipal. How then do critical reasons function?

F.R. Leavis[12] describes Henry James' *The Europeans* as a 'comparative inquiry' into the 'criteria of civilisation'. This very general and sweeping assessment of the central theme of the novel is about as paradigmatic a case of an interpretative judgement as one could wish for. Now Leavis' reasons for making this judgement operate on at least two levels. The lower level consists merely of recounting of the plot and some quotation of the novel's dialogue. Of course, there is an important element of selection, particularly in the latter. The slightly raffish Felix suggests that Clifford Wentworth and Felix's married sister Eugenia should form an attachment so as to wean Clifford from drink. Mr Wentworth is rather shocked. Leavis takes this as a humorous confrontation of New World Puritanism with the values of the Old World. This judgement I would describe as interpretative but such a judgement is less controversial than the very summary thesis with which I began. So the structure of the reasoning takes us inductively from quite uncontested judgements about the detail of the novel via judgements about the meaning of episodes to an overall view, though not, unfortunately, always in that order. So an interpretation needs to be worked in this way through to the detail of the novel, play or poem, and the interpretation of the detail must be both plausible and consistent with the overall view taken. In the example from Leavis the structure is in general reasonably clear. The values bound up with living a civilised life differ for Felix and Mr Wentworth, and how they differ is seen in their separate reactions to the problems of Clifford's attachment to the bottle. The hermeneutic circle appears in the way the critic exhibits, through his selection of detail and his understanding of the minutiae, the general interpretation he wishes to advance.

Such a general interpretation thus depends upon a particular impression of the work in which certain passages, sub-themes and parts of the plot stand out in the reader's mind: in one's memory of a novel, the plot and a few highlights stand out, the rest is lost. To use the fashionable jargon we owe to the Prague Structuralists,[13] certain elements are foregrounded. This synoptic impression is primitive in the aetiology of the development of an interpretation; from here it is that the process most often begins. I shall call this synoptic impression the 'reading' of a work. (The term is assumed to apply quite generally to arts other than literature for in all of them the process of foregrounding and backgrounding is important.) These passages which so dominate our impression of the work are either those passages which we find especially fascinating or interesting in some way, or they are the passages that give us particular pleasure.

The reading thus links the interpretation with the enjoyment of the work and prevents the former from being a purely intellectual and cerebral affair with no connection with the more sensuous side of our experience of art. It is the reading which records what takes my attention about the work.

If I read a critic's interpretation of the work he may lead my attention to passages in the work which I may not have foregrounded and due reflection on which may enhance my appreciation of the work. So in this way another's interpretation may change my experience of the work by drawing my attention to different episodes. If I endorse an interpretation which reflects my own reading, whether the interpretation was originally mine or not, then I take the first step towards ordering and making clear my experience of the work of art. Finally, of course, I may read an interpretation before reading, hearing or seeing the work, and the interpretation may influence my initial contact with the work. These are, I suppose, the three most common ways in which the reading and the interpretation of a work of art will be related.

One interesting feature about this is that whereas our 'reading' of a work of art may change in this way, it does not follow that our overall assessment of its merits or demerits necessarily will. The effect of reading criticism may well be to change the net impression of a work. When it is effective, the image one has of the work collapses and re-forms like the image in a kaleidoscope, with a hitherto neglected element taking on a new importance against the rest of the work. At one time it was the opening of Brahms' *G Major String Sextet* which particularly held my attention, but latterly it is the coda to the first movement. Yet though my preferences for certain sections within the work have changed, my overall impression of the work's stength has not. I would still rate it much as I rated it a decade or so ago. An analogy is perhaps to be found in the way that one's original reasons for believing something to be the case may change in favour of new reasons without our ceasing to think the proposition in question true; I might be told by somebody what 'pleonasm' means and then read its definition in the dictionary; it would be natural for my knowledge to be subsequently supported by my knowledge of the dictionary rather than word-of-mouth.

In the light of all this we can better understand the role played by the teacher in aesthetic education. The student of physics, philosophy or pharmacy does not have to find his studies pleasurable or interesting; it helps if he does, of course, but it is not a necessary condition for success. But a teacher of literature will feel that he has failed if the student, though competent in his handling of the critical techniques (he can spot half-rhymes, alliteration, etc.) remains unmoved by the poem. The same is true of the teacher of art or music. Ideally the student does not merely enjoy the work in question and find through this enjoyment his own reading, but he needs also to form an interpretation that reflects this reading. The interpretation may be a copy of his teachers or of some critic he has read; when he reads the poem or listens to the music with that interpretation guiding the relative importance he attaches to the various sections then his reading becomes a token of a type which is explained in terms of the interpretation. On this occasion his interpretation is similarly a token of that general type. Thus the type-token distinction applies to the broader sense of interpretation in much the same way that it applies to the performing arts, a thesis I argued in Chapter 2. Now we can see, through the relation between the reading and the interpretation, how the teacher can help the student both to enjoy and understand. It is not enough for the student to be able to list mechanically the devices the artist uses. Then his interpretation will not relate to an experience of the work which is in any way vivid or personal; it is not genuinely his own interpretation but merely one which he has acquired in a quite cerebral way. Even if his pleasure and interest in what he foregrounds is guided by his mentor, his aesthetic reaction to the work is no longer merely intellectual as it would be if what he foregrounds is picked out only because it plays a certain role in a preferred interpretation. It is necessary that the passages should be found enjoyable or interesting by the reader or listener himself. When the critic points out certain passages, perhaps by quoting them or playing them, he offers us a reading. Some philosophers have thought that this is all there is to art criticism; it is certainly fundamental but I have argued that it is only a starting-point; from it we spin our interpretative web.

Now the model of explanatory reasoning which has dominated English-speaking philosophy has been based on what philosophers believed scientific reasoning to be. General statements were thought to be either derived from or testable by independent particular observations. Despite the erosion of this approach during the last two decades through the attack on the law-deductive theory of explanation and the general realisation that the obser-vations that test a theory must be couched in terms of that theory and cannot be independent of it, the existence of an alternative hermeneutical theory of explanation deriving from the German philosopher Dilthey has not been fully appreciated. The theory given in this chapter fits much more happily into that tradition. The critic does select and he may place on one side elements in a story which seem to accord ill with the general thesis he wishes to advocate. This is not necessarily reprehensible. Any novel or any large-scale piece of imaginative literature contains a diversity of elements. It defines a possible world. A reading inevitably takes some sections as being of greater significance than others; this is part and parcel of the critical activity. Forming a view of the work requires taking some elements into the foreground and placing some in the background and it is out of this activity that interpretations grow. Equally a critic's selection reflects his own deepest commitments. A Marxist and a Christian reader may view *Jane Eyre* differently.

Exactly the same process of foregrounding and back grounding is to be found in our response to the other arts — to music, film or painting. It is this broader sense of interpretation which unifies our experience of the arts, for we shall find that the other form of interpretation we distinguished at the outset, interpretation in the performing arts, obeys the same principles. We require of a satisfying interpretation that the general conception of the work is carried through down to the detail. The interpretation needs to be consistent through and through. If the pianist regards the slow movement of the *Waldstein* as a mere link between the two substantial movements then it must be played lightly and rapidly and there can be no lingering on a particular phrase which he finds attractive. He must resist the temptation to make those final bars too soulful.

Dilthey also introduced the concept of the *Einsdruck-spunkt* (impression point), a moment of illumination around which the interpretation can be built. Such a moment, like the conversion of St Augustine, can give meaning to the whole of a man's life as well as to a work of art. Kermode suggests, rightly, that there may be more than one such point of entry into a work, and it is certainly possible that a reading which foregrounds a particular element may be consistent with more than one interpretation. Thus Tillyard and Woodhouse agree that the final section of Milton's *Comus* is the climax, but disagree in their overall interpretation of the masque; one believes it to represent the triumph of chastity, and the other the triumph of grace. Equally the *Einsdruckspunkt* may be misleading in that there are other, ultimately more enriching, points of entry into the work. (By a more enriching point of entry, I mean a passage which, when foregrounded, can sustain an interpretation which gives greater coherence to the whole and which itself remains interesting and exciting on each return.)

In the main, it is the variety of foregroundings which a work can withstand on which ultimately depends the variety of interpretations which are possible. For if we can select from a number of possible readings in which different sections of the work are foregrounded, then various interpretations will answer to those various readings. Of course, some readings will be eccentric in as much as the consensus would reject them as defensible readings of the work. We have seen some examples. But amongst the valid approaches to a work may be a number of different readings, and it is in this possibility of selection that the idiosyncrasy of art criticism ultimately lies.

In what sense, then, can we speak of a critic as explaining a work of art to us? I think the form of this explanation is quite familiar. If one wishes to produce a work with this particular theme or general character, then producing a work with these features is one way of doing it. The episodes picked out are explained in a way which fits in with the general form of explanations of action i.e. anybody with this aim might choose this as a way of bringing it about. What is important here is that works of art need to be conceived as the products of intentional action in order for this particular form of explanation to get under way. Now to say this is not to say that the author intended that the work should bear this interpretation, nor that this particular reading is correct because the author endorsed it. The reference is to a possible creative mind and this mirrors my preferred form of intentionalism, that the meaning of the literary text is to be found in a meaning or meanings that the author *could* have intended to convey (writing at the time and the place and in the language that he did).

Before examining the question of metaphor, which raises in little many of the issues we have been discussing, let us reflect briefly on the lessons this analysis of interpretation in art holds. It gives us additional reasons for rejecting the conception of art as essentially being a form of expression. In the performing arts, and Expressionism has been a theory which has always seemed especially appropriate to the performing arts, the character a work has in performance depends upon the interpreter. Is the slow movement of the *Eroica* sad? It depends on the interpreter whether it is sad or hysterical. It certainly is not gay music but within the constraints of the notes its interpreted character will vary.

The second general theory of aesthetics for which this account of interpretation raises difficulties is that art is a means of communicating certain of the creator's ideas to the audience. This view, a cousin to Expressionism, finds many supporters. But the presumption behind the arguments of this chapter is that the work of art is an object for interpretation and not a hermetic means of communication. Since artists choose ways of communicating that involve the audience in energetic feats of analysis and comprehension, if art were really a form of communication, it would be odd that artists should sometimes choose to make things so difficult for their public. They do not always do so, of course, but works which are suitable for interpretation are usually complex. The usual reason given for this apparent perversity is that what is to be communicated can only be communicated in that particular way. But if we think that works of art are at least frequently if not invariably works designed for the exercise of interpretative skills then this ceases to be a puzzle and its solution is no longer required.

The final misconception, now fortunately less popular than it was once, is that aesthetic attention is comtemplative in character. Providing contemplation is not supposed to imply passivity but allows the active use of the imagination in the reading and interpreting of art, this is perhaps harmless but frequently aesthetic experience is thought to be a unstrenuous affair. Enough has been said here to show the implausibility of this particular prejudice.

THE INTERPRETATION OF METAPHOR

Middleton Murray once remarked that the investigation of metaphor takes one to the borderline of sanity; this perhaps pardonable piece of hyperbole might seem more justified when we survey the subdivision of metaphor into those very unmemorable sub-species such as synecdoche, metonomy and the even more forgettable metalepsis and hyperbaton, the classification into which occupies books on rhetoric. However, I shall steal and rework one idea from classical sources and that is the distinction between utilitarian and decorative uses of metaphor. The traditional distinction saw the utilitarian function as a means of providing, through the rhetorical device known as catachresis, new words where new words are required. Much of the vocabulary we use to describe the workings of the mind, for example, has quite obviously metaphorical sources. We speak of somebody as having a probing or incisive mind, for example, and though these are now dead metaphors, their origin is quite clear. The idea of an incisive mind as 'cutting through difficulties' passed by the process of catachresis into literal usage and thus fills a gap by providing a word where one did not exist before. The colour words, 'mink' and 'cherry' are more obvious examples.

However the use I shall make of the terms marks a different distinction and one which is very closely related to the theme of this chapter, the interpretation of art. For I wish to distinguish the use of metaphor in an imaginative way where the reader is being invited to interpret what the text says and the use of metaphor to ornament or decorate a statement which directly conveys information. Although many writers have stressed the 'openness' of metaphor, indeed Beardsley describes them as 'miniature poems', fewer writers have remarked upon their ornamental usage, though Black does draw attention to it in his more recent work on the subject. However my concern will mainly be with what I shall cut their 'essential use'.

The starting-point for modern discussions of metaphor has been Max Black's earlier essay which first appeared in the 1950s.[14] Since it owes something in turn to I.A. Richards' work, the general ideas may not be too unfamiliar. Black proposes what he calls an 'interaction theory' which is designed to replace those theories which regard metaphor as merely disguised simile, which he designates 'comparison' or 'substitution' theories. (The former is a special case of the latter and does not seem to merit the special attention that Black gives it. In brief, Black's account of metaphor runs as follows:

1   Metaphors are statements which contain both a principal and subsidiary subject or system of subjects.
2   There exists a stock of commonplace beliefs which hold for the subsidiary subject: these provide us with material from which we, by a process of filtering, extract those propositions which are true of the subsidiary subject and are also illuminatingly applied to the principal subject. The result is a shift in meaning of the words involved in the metaphorical system.

Thus a metaphor such as 'That man is a lion' we read armed with certain commonplaces about lions, such as that they are strong, courageous, dangerous, four-footed, carnivorous and covered with fur. From these we select those characteristics which hold also for the man in question. He may not travel on all fours, be covered in fur, and he may be a vegetarian, but the metaphor is justified if he is strong and courageous. Note that the commonplaces do not have to be true; for example, the use of 'a wolf' in metaphor has been dictated by certain commonplaces which are false. They are apparently amiable, faithful to their mates, affectionate in looking after their cubs and, like most wild animals but unlike man, they kill only when they need food. None of these facts operates when we describe a man as a wolf in sheep's clothing. The lupine characteristics we are attributing are rapacity, disloyalty, unreliability, viciousness, etc. which are not in fact true of wolves in the wild but were traditionally ascribed to them.

To dispose of one or two common mistakes first of all. Both Damaan and Davidson argue, surely correctly, that there is no case for saying that words change their meaning when they enter metaphors. If they did then putting a word into a metaphor would change its sense to one which we would have to guess, presumably from what the metaphor says or could be saying. All metaphors would then be disguised definitions of the words being used metaphorically. But the force of a metaphor depends, even on Black's own analysis, on our bringing to the metaphor the usual and standard meaning of these words. And, *en passant*, Damaan is equally justified in objecting to the widespread myth that metaphors are somehow an aesthetically more powerful device than similes. It is odd to find Stanford echoing this in a book which simultaneously notes the relative paucity of metaphors in Homer.

In his recent paper, 'More about Metaphor', Black stresses that when we interpret metaphor we handle a system of ideas associated with the subsidiary subject rather than simply a single referring term. Consequently, interpretation emerges in the form of a set of assertions correlated on the one hand with 'wolf', and on the other hand with 'man' in such a way that we construct a set of parallels between the two. However it still remains rather unclear why Black calls his theory an 'Interaction Theory', for there is in fact no interaction. It is the subject of the metaphor alone and not the predicate which appears differently to us in the metaphorical context. Admittedly Black suggests that to call a man a wolf puts the wolf in a special light as well as the man in that it draws out human characteristics of the wolf, but there seems no reason to think that the action of metaphor is reciprocal in this way. Black does not subsequently make very much of it and I am inclined to think that the name 'Interaction Theory' is not well chosen.

According to Black's summary of his theory, we select certain commonplaces from a stock which apply to the subsidiary subject and then use these to ascribe the relevant characteristics to the principal subject. The first major objection is that it is often mistaken to think that, in interpreting a metaphor, we are reliant upon a stock of commonplaces. Sometimes, and very often in the case of vivid metaphor, it is a question of reaching around for something which can be predicted of the principal sub-ject. The solution reached under the constraints of the context need not be drawn from commonplaces at all. The construing of a metaphor is an exercise which, at its best, requires a high degree of skill and imagination. Of course, I may find a metaphor stunning without being able to say quite why and quite what could be asserted by it. But this, as Eliot remarked, is characteristic of poetry and, I would add, of the arts in general.

Look again at Empson's gloss on Shakespeare's metaphor 'bare ruined choirs' as a description of Autumn woods. Is it a commonplace that choirs consist of tall pillars, a characteristic that can be filtered out and applied to a ruined religious house? The answer is that it is only some choirs which bear this relationship to some forests. It is not an analogy which would strike one between a tropical rain forest and a church, or between a Romanesque choir and any forest. Rain forests are too tangled and Romanesque churches have pillars that are too fat and stubby. What we are interested in is whether some choirs resemble some woods, and it is this that is the basis upon which the metaphor works. It is not true that we select from a set of commonplaces, for common places are true or assumed true of the entire class in question. The operation of metaphor is more particular than Black imagines; we are concerned with whether one particular forest could look like a church, not in terms of the general characteristics of forests so much as in the possibility of there being a forest which looked like this. We cannot check the wood or the abbey that Shakespeare had in mind; in any case either or both might have been imaginary, and the metaphor still be effective.

Look at another example, Macbeth's 'Sleep that knits up the ravell'd sleave of care'. There is an element of personification here as there often is in metaphor. Like, I suspect, most modern readers I thought of the unravelling of the sleeve of a sweater and the metaphor certainly works given those associations. But when I checked I found that 'sleave' probably refers to the end of silks that silk-workers find it difficult to finish. Clearly this brings different associations to bear; those things which, try as we may, we remain anxious about and unable to settle satisfactorily are the things which sleep heals. As against this the modern reader would come to the image with associations of frayed nerves. So the understanding of this metaphor in terms of what the author would have intended needs not so much a repertoire of common-places as some pretty specialised knowledge for which we need the scholar. So the thesis Black proposes will at least have to be rephrased as referring to commonplaces available at the time of writing. Even then I doubt whether it is true. I do not know, and perhaps nobody knows, how widely the processes of silk manufacture were known in Elizabethan England, but it is perfectly feasible to suppose that many metaphors require quite specialised knowledge. It is unreasonable to think of a poet as stopping to ensure that his metaphor relies on commonplaces before he writes the next line. Black's analysis begins to look like an analysis of tired and stale metaphor. A vivid metaphor may offer something to the general reader but so much more to the reader who shares certain esoteric knowledge with the writer. Steiner puts this well:

A poet can crowd his idiom, his landscape of motion, with the minutiae of history of locale, of technical process (a key passage in Hamlet turns on the arcane technicalities of dyeing). He can cram hell, purgatory and paradise with gossip so private that elucidation depends on an almost street-by-street intimacy with thirteenth-century Florence.[15]

It is often said that metaphors are nonsense when con-strued literarily (if 'literary' usage can be contrasted with metaphorical here without question-begging). It is nonsense, what Ryle called a category mistake, to think of Sleep knitting. (Is sleep a good knitter, fast or slow, what size needles is he using, and is he knitting one plain one purl?) Aristotle's observation that in metaphor a word is applied to something which is not its proper subject might seem to encourage this though it is also compatible with the idea that metaphors are simply false. Indeed, as a matter of fact many metaphors are simply contingently false. If I describe a bass as singing with his mouth full of turtle soup, the recognition of the appro-priateness of this description of the sound he produces depends upon seeing that the description of him is false. He is not exactly singing with his mouth full of soup, if this is a possibility. (If a ventriloquist can talk whilst drinking a glass of beer, then presumably a bass might be able to sing Prince Gremin's aria[15] from *Eugene Onegin* whilst drinking turtle soup.) Since we assume that he is not, we can attend to the metaphor as a way of characterising the sound; the singer sounds as if his mouth is shut and he is afraid to open it in case Onegin is drenched. But it would be a mistake to suppose, as Beardsley does, that all metaphors are false. Some are true. A student of mine suggested Donne's 'No man is an island'; 'He's no angel' is another. Equally one can easily think of examples where a true statement is made in a context where the speaker makes it clear that the statement refers to a third party in a metaphorical manner. Imagine that I hear of a politician retiring before a scandal breaks; I remark to my neighbour, 'Old foxes always seek their holes when they suspect danger'. My statement, taken literally, is true as far as I know. It is still a metaphorical comment on the news. Many metaphors are, of course, obviously false or perhaps obviously nonsense. Some recent examples which have occurred in philosophical discussion are 'Marriage is a zero sum game', 'Men are verbs not nouns', Ezra Pound's 'Educators are sheep-herders'. A favourite of my own is e.e. cummings' 'A politician is an arse upon which every one has sat except a man'. All of these are false or nonsensical if taken straight; consequently the metaphor forces upon the reader the need to consider what sort of idea could be communicated by a sentence so obviously deviant. It demands interpretation and the exercise of the reader's imagination. What could be said by a statement which so blatantly contravenes the convention that assertion is used to convey truths? But the same sort of impetus to interpretation could be achieved by uttering the obviously irrelevant or even the obviously trivial (though irony is more usual in the latter case).

Much the same applies to similes: these tend to be vacuously true when taken 'straight'. In his *Orchid Trilogy* Jocelyn Brooke, misquoting Huxley likens the laugh of one of his characters, Mercaptan, in *Antic Hay*, to an orchestra of bulls and canaries. Since one can always find some point of likeness, this is trivially true if it is not taken as an invitation to interpret. Both are sounds, both made by living creatures and so on. If we expand the simile into what Damaan calls 'a literal comparison statement' then we have a statement of the form 'x is like y in respects a, b, c, etc.' which is now true or false in a nonvacuous way. Thus if I said, 'His laugh is like the sound which would be made by an orchestra of bulls and canaries where each animal produced its characteristic sound antiphonally' then I shall have spelled out the simile as a literal comparison, and one which will be either true or false. Incidentally what is so comic about this superb simile is its visual element. For the full flavour of Brooke's improvement we need to imagine bulls and canaries sitting behind orchestra desks of the sort used by a jazz big band. The extent to which metaphors need to be visualised is moot; the description of metaphors and similes as 'images' seems to commend the attempt to picture them, but this is clearly easier with some metaphors than others. I can see how this simile may be visualised or indeed Pound's 'educators are sheepherders' might be, but I cannot see how to represent 'Marriage is a zero-sum game' as a private cartoon. However the insight which makes philosophers look for falsity in a metaphor is a sound one. In Empson's phrase 'metaphors are pregnant'. Falsity is one way of forcing us to look past the surface meaning so as to detect those associations which hold for both terms. Reading a metaphor requires an act of skill in elucidation by the reader, and is just one more way in which art demands an active participation by the public. They are moves in a teasing game played by the writer with or against his reader. In Coleridge's words, 'You feel him to be a poet in as much as, for a time, he has made you one – an active creative being'.

I can put the thesis schematically as follows: imagine that a metaphor is read twice; on first reading it is dismissed as false or trivial, or as nonsense. This invites a second reading; on reconsideration, the reader looks for an interpretation such that the author can be thought to be drawing some enlightening comparison between the various objects mentioned. Context, of course, invites us to step past the first stage and attempt an imaginative reading. Why can we not just substitute the reading for the original metaphor? Black is surely right in his answer to this question. 'The implications, previously left for a suitable reader to educe for himself, with a nice feeling for their relative priorities and degrees of importance, are now presented explicitly as though having equal weight', though one needs to add the caveat that he is surely wrong to speak of 'implications' here.

In his most recent paper on the subject, Black imagines a game which has evolved from chess which he calls 'epichess'. In epichess a player can move a piece as though it had the value of any other piece the mover nominates just as long as his opponent accepts that move. (Any competent player would, of course, veto any really effective use of such a ploy, but that does not matter for the purposes of the argument.) Such a game is a model of how metaphor works; any move in discourse is meaningful if a competent speaker of the language will accept it. The analogy is both intriguing and illuminating, but it does overlook a distinction between two sorts of writer; we can describe a writer as playing a game with or against his readers. Within imaginative literature we might think of Donne, Eliot and Joyce as writing against their readers and of Pope, Dryden and George Eliot, with most writers of fiction, as writing with their readers. The difference is in the extent to which the writer sets his readers problems rather than takes him with them in a joint voyage of exploration and discovery. But this contrast, agreeable though it is, is misleading in one vital respect. For I want to propose that the use of metaphor in imaginative writing generally, whether it is prose or verse, is significantly different from the use of metaphors in much scientific writing, history, philosophy, political speeches, literary criticism or epitaphs. Their use in imaginative writing is essential whereas their use in the latter sorts of writing is ornamental.

I have argued that the importance of metaphor as a literary device lies in its openness. It reflects in microcosm the general characteristic of imaginative literature. Imaginative literature, I claim, does not contain general truths about human nature so much as offer scope for their generation. So is it proper to speak, as Black does, of metaphors as a species of statement? The answer is that it depends upon the context. A metaphor whose function is ornamental is merely a more attractive way of stating a fact and is thus a statement in ear-catching dress; such metaphors are paraphrasable and are thus utilitarian rather than essential.

The writer of common or garden prose uses metaphors simply to enliven; they are not devices which extend the reader's participation by allowing him to interpret them in a wide variety of ways so that the entire piece can bear in consequence a variety of different meanings. Instead they are replaceable by a literal construction without prejudice to the meaning of the whole. In this final salvo against Black I return to the main theme; in imaginative literature, the metaphor offers, not a statement, but an occasion for their formulation.

However, put this way I give the impression that imaginative literature is alone in its use of essential metaphors which allow such scope for interpretation. That would be, I think, an oversimplification. We have recently come to realise the role which metaphors play in other areas of human endeavour, such as science and religion. Whether the limitations on the understanding of a metaphor such as the description of atoms in terms of miniature solar systems or talk of an electron cloud are more exacting than in literary metaphor is controversial. Some metaphors are easily cashable in terms of literal comparisons but it is highly likely that a metaphor such as 'the brain is a computer' is open to a great variety of plausible interpretations at the present time. In such cases it may be as difficult to decide whether a given understanding of the metaphor lies within or outside scientific tradition as it is to decide whether a certain controversial interpretation of a literary metaphor is compatible with what we know of the literary culture in which it originated. In the case of a religious metaphor such as 'Christ is the Lamb of God' there are perhaps more clear indications as to what orthodoxy permits as a permissible interpretation. Consequently these fall nearer to what I describe as the ornamental use of metaphors. The details of the use of metaphor in science and religion are beyond our scope here. Suffice to say that ornamental and essential usages represent two poles within which metaphor may move, whether the context is a poem, a scientific report or a religious homily.

CONCLUSION

The openness to interpretation of a literary work of art requires the use of verbal devices which will not exclude the possibility of their sustaining a multiplicity of different readings. Such a possibility is, of course, not normally intended by the historian, philosopher, or critic. If the politician is in the game of systematic ambiguity this is not generally valued by the rest of us no matter how much it may be admired by politicians. The difference is between a mode of discourse of which our primary expectation is that it is truth-bearing and a mode of discourse where the primary intention is to create artefacts which may be interpreted in various ways by the reader. Qua imaginative writer the novelist is not primarily concerned to convey truths. There is no such person as Samuel Pickwick and if Malleson in *Women in Love* is modelled on Bertrand Russell it is a factor we ignore when we appraise the novel. A writer may, of course, choose a certain person or character as the vehicle of his own views; but once the relation of the authorial voice to that character becomes unambiguous, art has turned into propaganda. In my view this happens from time to time in Lawrence and, of course, in Tolstoy's later writings. There is no harm in the author using one or more characters to convey his own comments provided the reader does not know. He may suspect, of course, and such suspicions are of the essence of imaginative reading but the author must not let the reader's suspicions harden into knowledge.

6

Comparative Judgement

To works not raised upon principles demonstrative and scientific, but appealing wholly to observation and experience, no other test can be applied than length of duration and continuance of esteem (Samuel Johnson, *Preface to Shakespeare*).

If one of the major tasks for the critic is the interpretation of art, the other is surely its evaluation. It would certainly be naïve to insist on a sharp distinction between the two. The very selection of a work of art for interpretation betokens the judgement that it is meritorious. We just do not bother with mediocre work. Great art offers so much more scope to the interpreter. But as well as evaluation by implication, we look to the critic for an assessment of the relative standing of different works and it is easily understandable that we should do so. *Ars longa, vita brevis*; who would choose to spend hours of a short life in the pursuit of the meretricious. Much art, of course, we readily dismiss as unworthy of our attention because its failings are immediately apparent. Where we need the help of the critic is in the case of art which is worthy and competent but dull, for this is the art whose technical proficiency suggests that our initial boredom might be the result of too shallow an acquaintance. It is not always easy to distinguish art which is ultimately rewarding and art which is ultimately dull. Brownings's dramatic monologue *Andrea del Sarto* purports to be by a man whose art is technically accomplished (the sub-title of the poem is *Called the Faultless Painter*) yet lacks the inspiration of Raphael or Michaelangelo. Of a work of the former the painter says

That arm is wrongly put — and there again —
A fault to pardon in the drawing's lines,
Its body, so to speak: its soul is right,
He means right — that, a child may understand.
Still, what an arm! and I could alter it.
But all the play, the insight and the stretch —
Out of me! Out of me!

Such evaluative judgements are often described as judgements of taste. In classifying them so, we place them with judgements about food and drink rather than with moral or perceptual judgements. Disputes about perception are more easily concluded. We may disagree about whether a distant figure is the prime minister, but such a judgement can be settled: we can get closer, ask a policeman, or an aide, and so on. But if we disagree as to whether Berlioz is a great composer worthy to be placed beside Verdi and Mozart the methods of settling such a dispute are much more obscure; indeed, we may quite rapidly reach pure confrontation. Yet the very existence of that confrontation suggests that these judgements are different from judgements about food or wine where there seems very little scope for anything more than a recognition that you like the taste of game, say, whereas I do not. Cyril Ray or André Simon may be better judges of food and wine than you or me, but there seems no grounds for saying that jugged hare is 'really' delicious because they say so. There are simply individual tastes which may be cultivated or not.

We do not take the same view of aesthetic judgement. Not only are there cultivated tastes in the arts, but furthermore we believe, unless we are playing at aesthetic scepticism, that Mozart is 'really' a better composer than Reger, and Keats 'really' a better poet than Byron. Admittedly the differences which still remain between one man's taste and another do not generally worry us nearly as much as parallel differences over moral judgement. I might regret or even despise the man who prefers Hemingway to Conrad, but I do not regard him with the horror that I reserve for the man who maintains that birth control is morally wrong or that hanging is justifiable. Differences over aesthetic judgements are more important than differences of taste in vegetables, but less important than differences of moral judgement.

How then can I differentiate between my private likes and dislikes and the status of a writer or composer? How can I concede that Wagner or Gerard Manly Hopkins are great creative artists whilst finding their work unattractive? How can I prefer Janacek to Brahms, whilst allowing that the latter is the more significant figure? In what follows I shall defend a form of the assent or consensus theory of judgement; but before I do, there are some more fundamental questions to be considered.

> 'It is only an auctioneer who can equally and
> impartially admire all art' (Oscar Wilde).

The thesis that the comparative judgement of art is not governed by rules is a thesis which, though it has had its critics recently, still commands wide support. In part the plausibility of this thesis derives from the quite signal lack of success which critics and pedagogues have had in formulating general rules which state the conditions under which a work of art is good or bad. If we look through the history of music, for example, we find that the rules which govern classical sonata form were formulated after the first great achievements in that style, and that even then great composers such as Haydn went their own way. Standard textbooks used to specify that there should be two themes or groups of themes, the first of which should be assertive in the tonic or home key, and the second a more lyrical section in the dominant. But Haydn frequently composed monothematic movements in which the second group of material was thematically related to the first. Equally the rules which govern harmonic progression, for example that consecutive fifths and octaves were to be avoided, were broken in works of genuine and even outstanding merit. It would be idle to pretend that the rules of traditional harmony and counterpoint are rules which the composer breaks at his peril. Works composed consistently with them may be dull, and works of great value ignore them. Somebody was unwise enough to remark to Beethoven that a certain sequence was not allowed, at which the great composer thundered, 'Well I allow it'. More gently Haydn remarked that these were matters for the ear to judge, and his ear was as good as anybody else's. Perhaps the whole matter is best summed up in the story about Gainsborough's painting the Blue Boy in order to refute Reynold's principle that a successful picture could not be predominantly blue. Rules are a challenge to the master of the next generation. All this suggests that the search for critical criteria based on these conditions is pointless. But perhaps there are stronger arguments.

It is often held that works of art are unique. This uniqueness is much touted, but the concept itself is elusive. After all, it will be said, every material object is unique in being distinct from any other. Aesthetic uniqueness is presumably stronger than this, for it is assumed that we are making a claim about works of art which is not true of other objects. One strong form of the thesis is, I think, disputable. It is sometimes argued that a work of art is such that any change or cut will alter or destroy its aesthetic value by changing its aesthetic properties. Works of art are thus much more different from even superficially similar works: behind this is the ideal of a work of art so completely unified that a change in only part destroys its internal coherence. However, this might not be true of the majority of even highly regarded works. The dropping of a sentence or the changing of punctuation in *Madame Bovary* might make very little difference to the novel; Flaubert was such a careful craftsman that the punctuation was, no doubt, considered but it is implausible to suppose that a small change will have very large repercussions even though it might reduce the aesthetic impact of the sentence in question. Anyway, the aesthetic properties of dynamism, gracefulness, and so on are rather more robust than this thesis supposes. We should bear in mind, too, both the great variety of forms of art and the numerous works that are widely read, seen or heard though in an unfinished or flawed state. However the thesis can be read with some plausibility as a disguised recommendation to the critic to pay attention to the detail and in this form is surely salutary.

I shall follow philosophical practice in linking the concept of uniqueness[1] with questions of value and criterion for it is in this context that the question has traditionally been raised. The two quotations which follow exemplify the tradition:

For every work of art is unique and in the last resort, perhaps, can be judged by no other standard but its own.

The more radical arguments against critical standards are spread out in the pages of Croce, Dewey, Richards, Prall and the great Romantic critics before them ... in one way or another they all attempt to expose the absurdity of presuming to judge a work of art, the very excuse for whose existence lies in its *difference* from everything that has gone before it, by its degree of *resemblance* to something that has gone before; and on close inspection they create at least a very strong doubt as to whether a standard of success or failure in art is either necessary or possible.[2]

If we pursue the possibility of making alterations in a work like *Madame Bovary*, we rapidly run up against the difficulty that a copy or another version of a work of art cannot count as a work of art in its own right. So there is not the possibility of grouping together similar objects in a class so that they share the same good-making characteristics. If we are deciding, for example, what makes a knife a good knife – its sharpness, the grip of the handle and its balance, etc. – we can use these characteristics to select from a group of knives all those which are good knives, and there is no limit to the number which may qualify. Now if I group together a number of copies of a poem I have not produced a parallel situation: they are all the same poem. The same applies to recordings of an interpretation of a symphony. If, on the other hand, I make a few small alterations in the wording in each copy whose effect is minimal, the results are still not separate poems which have roughly the same merit as the original, but simply versions of the first. The same goes for versions of a symphony. Bruckner's revisions count as versions of the same symphony: Brahms' later revision of the *Op. 8 Trio* is not a different work sufficiently similar to have the same good-making characteristics which made us view the earlier version as a masterpiece. It is simply a version differing mainly in concision. The important and indeed crucial point is that where two works are sufficiently similar to be judged good on the basis of certain features which they hold in common they are not distinct works of art. It is in this that the especial uniqueness of works of art lies. Now it is certainly not impossible that two distinct works of art may have merits in common. For example, different works are separately praised for their unity. The problem, as Hume saw so clearly, is that where such criteria are precise they exclude good works and where they are not they are useless in the practice of criticism.

It is then the uniqueness of works of art that makes criteria of so little use in critical judgement. The unsurprising nature of this revelation emerges when we consider what would happen if we could establish such criteria. We could then teach these criteria to apprentices in our academies and produce works of art of merit at the drop of a hat. But to suppose that we could produce works of art as a cook produces soufflés according to the recipe book is obviously absurd, and it is absurd primarily because we look for an original addition to a tradition in art. Part of what distinguishes art from craft is the fact that a work of art attempts both to update and continue a tradition of art. For this to happen that work must be original; its uniqueness trivially follows.

Now it might still be argued that, on the contrary, there are well known rules and principles which every artist has to study in acquiring mastery. I have already referred to the classical rules of counterpoint, harmony and form in music and there are parallel rules in the writing of verse. Welsh verse, in particular, has a number of classical forms and metres. Few achieve distinction without a thorough mastery of these traditional forms. Of course, adherence to orthodox forms may result in a boringly academic work, or it may produce a masterpiece like *Eine*

Kleine Nachtmusik, a paradigm of classical sonata form. This then leaves a good deal of latitude for the critic, for a work may be good or middling despite its adherence to strict forms. Judged in terms of a particular style a work may or may not succeed according to the extent to which it satisfies the rules for that style. So at least, then, it looks as though we have some guidance for the critic through minimum standards of competence and thus a counter-argument to the sort of position I have advocated.

However, a great artist may, it is often claimed, make or break the rules of his art in a way that a lesser artist may not. The rules of harmonic progression and sonata form were often broken by Schubert's extravagant modulations but his cavalier treatment of the rules usually had an artistic point. Arthur Hutchings has this to say about the Great C major symphony,

Among the claimants for the honour of being the composer of the greatest symphony is there any but Schubert who offers a specimen in which the purpose is so integral yet the manner so diffuse? Even the introductory slow tune, having been presented with lovely orchestral variations, sets off on a burgeoning development which every student knows does not belong there – except in this work; and as it is meant for this work, what fool would call it misplaced?[3]

Sometimes then the rules governing sonata form are ignored with successful results even if, in general, failure to observe the rules damages the structure of the work. The problem facing the critic is now to determine when the rules cease to be applicable to a work because that work transcends them. It must be obvious that such a decision implies an evaluation of the work which cannot itself be criterion-governed because we cannot judge that a work transcends the rules in terms of those rules. Therefore to decide that the rules do not apply is to make an evaluative decision that cannot itself be rule-governed; for given some rules of a higher level, their application would still have to be decided. So much could in any case be inferred from the fact that such rules are invariably the *post hoc* formulations of the procedure of an earlier generation of composers. Of course it is true that, when called upon, we can usually give reasons for critical judgement but such judgements tend to rely on picking out features which are themselves either graded implicitly through being selected or are explicitly described in value-terms.

These consequences follow from the arguments that I presented earlier in this chapter. They make it very difficult to accept as a list of critical canons Beardsley's 'unity', 'intensity' and 'complexity'. When Beardsley argues that disunity is always a reason for downgrading a work, we may well agree. The point is that the condition is trivial. If we find an overabundance of unity in a work we describe the work as monotonous. Unity is generally used as a grading term in art so it is hardly surprising that it is a reason for praising works. But we require more of a critical criterion than it should itself depend upon a grading term. To avoid a regress we require non-aesthetic terms which are sufficiently precise for their application to be straight forwardly learnt and not to require, in turn, the exercise of critical taste. But this, in the nature of the case, we cannot have.

I began this chapter by raising the question of how we can distinguish between the 'real' stature of a writer, composer or artist and my own particular taste. Neville Cardus never much cared for the music of Bach, but he recognised that Bach was a great composer. I find the novels of Dickens unbearably prolix and facetious, 'loose baggy monsters' in fact, but I recognise that Dickens was a great novelist. Of course, if there were criterial properties in virtue of which Dickens or Bach were creative artists of stature then there would be no problem about their 'objective status' though there might then be problems as to how any individual could fail to appreciate the fact. Still, explanations might be forthcoming just as there are explanations available when somebody fails to perceive that a surface is the colour it really is. But given that the search for criterial properties is vain, what can we say?

A widely accepted answer is that the 'real' or 'true' status of a work or of a creative artist is established by the consensus of critics as to its or his stature. Thus it is because the novels of Dickens are admired by many critics of experience and discernment that I recognise that my own taste is somewhat idiosyncratic. Hanslick was wrong about Liszt's *B Minor Sonata* when he described it as a 'musical monstrosity' and remarked 'who has heard that, and finds it beautiful, is beyond help'. The reason why we are so confident is because this work is accepted by performers, critics and public alike as a masterpiece. The reason why it is a great sonata lies, of course, in its musical properties, its melodic material, and perhaps above all, its structure. I am not advocating a form of aesthetic idealism. The features which a work possesses are what makes it a work of quality. But we recognise its status through the operation of the critical consensus over a period of time.

In summary, works of art have characteristics or qualities which, in the best cases, 'please' the connoisseur. These qualities cannot, however, be made the basis of a set of criteria which will guide our judgement. Any work of art contains very many features which jointly produce its effect on the listener; but any one might be absent from a fine work. We judge the 'objective' status of a work of art by the consensus of connoisseurs.

So far the account presented is what might be called a simple or naïve consensus or assent theory of critical judgement and it has, as I have implied, fairly widespread support. I propose to replace this account with what I shall call a complex theory of critical judgement. Essential to this account is an understanding of the concept of an artistic tradition and how that concept differs from the idea of a history. So a digression on this topic is required.

I conceive the history of an art as essentially the construction of a narrative which shows how the major figures in an art, for example, poets of quality, added to and modified the tradition, and shows, in the course of recounting innovations, what influences caused them to write in the style they did. This overall scheme dictates the inclusion or exclusion of writers whose stature is, by general consent, minor. In the performing arts the concept of a tradition is intimately connected with that of the repertoire for the repertoire largely, if not entirely, coincides with the tradition. I shall take the tradition to involve selecting from the history of the art those works whose value is generally agreed to be high; such works are normally found in the repertoire; not invariably, of course; sometimes they may be caviar to the general and sometimes require forces difficult or expensive to assemble. Equally, books may be out of print and paintings in private and inaccessible collections. Nevertheless, works which have a place in the tradition need to be known to the cognoscenti.

As I understand it, the idea of a tradition is close to the concept of an internal history of art which the Prague Structuralists inherited from the school of critics known as the Russian Formalists. This needs to be distinguished from the sort of history of art which lists influences, the inventors of stylistic fingerprints, and so on. If you read a history of nineteenth-century piano music, for example, you will find that Chopin was influenced by Hummel and Field amongst others. Very little music by Hummel and Field is played now; they are not much more than what Tovey used to call 'Interesting Historical Figures' though they are by no means as obscure as the Alberti whose sole claim to fame is the Alberti bass. But in the criticism of music their names are absent. When a critic comes to discuss the piano music of Chopin, the figures we read about are Bach, Brahms and Liszt, all of whom have a secure place in the repertoire. We are interested in a composer's relation to the other great musicians in the repertoire. The same could be exemplified in the history and criticism of literature and the history and criticism of painting. Lyly's *Euphues* is a good example of a historically important work of literature which nobody much reads and which is not mentioned in criticism. Its importance lies in its influence.

Why is the concept of tradition important? In *Tradition and the Individual Talent* Eliot writes of the individual author: 'You cannot value him alone; you must set him, for contrast and comparison, among the dead. I mean this as a principle of aesthetic, not merely historical, criticism'. Can we transfer this to the judgement of the art work rather than the artist and at the same time give it a more precise content? If I know at what point in the development of an art a particular work appeared I shall know in what ways, if any, it develops the tradition, what innovations the creator makes, and in what ways he expected his work to surprise and delight his public. If the recognition of these features is relevant to its appreciation, and I think few would deny that it is, then it is necessary to know where the work belongs in the tradition in order to 'respond' properly to it. The consequences of this thesis for the idea of 'practical criticism' or of confronting the 'innocent ear' with anonymous music are pretty clear; but were I to stress these I should be doing no more than stamping on the grave of recently buried critical practice. Of course, as Stanley Cavell points out, music may not merely continue a tradition, it may metaphorically comment on it. How else are we to understand John Cage's *Silent Music*, for example, where the pianist does not lay a finger on the keyboard for the duration of the piece? Equally poetry which consists of blank pages, or works of art which consist of a canvas painted in a uniform colour, are more vulgar gestures at a tradition than continuations of it. But the great bulk of art has a less controversial relation to a tradition. In both cases, however, understanding a work involves understanding this relation.

In addition, the more we know of a tradition the more rapidly we 'place' a work we are hearing, reading or seeing for the first time; once we 'place' it we know what to look for, and so the work becomes intelligible to us more quickly; we look for the commencement of the development section in a sonata form movement, are eager to see how the composer handles the coda, and so on. If we are reading a novel by Lawrence we note the innovation he brings to the delineation of character through the direct expression of that character's inner turmoil. No doubt we are sometimes unconscious of the operation of this 'placing' of a work. Nevertheless, I think it is an important, indeed crucial part of our reaction to a work of art because it affects the attention we pay to the various aspects of the work. This selective attention requires some discussion, and the Prague School of Structuralists, in their distinction between foregrounding and backgrounding, provide us with a terminology in which these essential distinctions can be made. If a phrase in a spoken language is used so that it does not draw attention to itself, then Mukarovsky describes it as part of the background. This he calls 'automatisation'. Foregrounding occurs where a word attracts attention. To make a word or a phrase stand out in this way, we may use syntax or vocabulary which is rare in ordinary spoken or written language or unusual in that context. Metaphors, provided they are newly minted, have this effect. Dead metaphors such as 'weighing the evidence' are so familiar as to become part of the background. The conclusion which occurs immediately to the reader is that poetic language is language in which the maximum foregrounding is obtained by using language which constantly draws attention to itself as language and not merely as a transparent medium through which the meaning can be instantly sighted. But this would be to ignore the function of literary style; a style of poetic utterance may become so widely used as to be itself background to more striking departures from it; the poetic language may itself be background to the individual achievements of a great poet who writes in that style. We need such a distinction to recognise the merits of Pope as against minor Augustan writers. This leads Mukarovsky to propose a hierarchy of dominant-subordinate elements in language. Poetic language may indeed be foreground relative to ordinary language but provide the background to the more individual achievements within that style. In certain respects some elements may be foreground at one time but background at another; a certain rhyming scheme may be striking in one poem but background in later poems written at a time at which that device has become merely another feature of the accepted style. And at various points in the development of art, a typical reader's net impression of a work will change; the face the work presents to a reader (what Roman Ingarden calls its 'concretion') will vary.

Since we do not order the groceries in recitative and aria nothing in music corresponds to the role of ordinary language in providing background to poetic utterance. But we can date music by means of its style and the style which is common to the music of a period may provide the background in terms of which the innovations of a master may be foreground. Our grasp of the tradition of music enables us to 'place' a work's innovatory features in a way which would be impossible if we had no knowledge of how music develops. We know, for example, that Beethoven advanced the language of music, providing a precedent for form on a larger scale and an increasing toleration of dissonance. He provided models for the most gifted of his successors. Mosco Carner and Gerald Abraham have shown how the slow movement of Beethoven's *Seventh* influenced the slow movements of Schubert's *C major*, Berlioz's *Harold in Italy* and Mendelssohn's *Italian.* Since the nineteenth century with a history of, amongst other things, the increasing toleration of dissonance, we must conclude that the background against which an individual work was heard was itself continually in motion.

Exactly the same holds for the other arts. Even such a young art as the cinema has a well-defined stylistic tradition which enables an informed cinema-goer to place a film within a few years of its release. The stylistic changes of the late 1950s and early 1960s led to more rapid and apparently 'disconnected' cutting so that the audiences could not rely on narrative cues in the way that earlier audiences did. A film-goer of the 1940s with no knowledge of the development of the tradition might find a current film incomprehensible. Musicians may compare this with a composer's use of 'unprepared' dissonance or modulations.

Again, and I do not think Mukarovsky expatiates on this

point, our view of a particular work may change as a consequence of other works encountered in between readings, viewings or hearings. Meyer recently remarked of a certain triadic motif in the Schubert *Octet,*

Schubert's use of this traditional pattern influences our understanding of its implications in Beethoven's music, just as its use in Beethoven's music modified our comprehension of Schubert.[4]

Having noticed the role this motif plays, it becomes foreground for the time being. We pick it out as of special note and relegate other material to the background. As a consequence of different interpretations, or of conversations with critics or friends, our impression of a work, its 'concretion', will vary. I discussed the relationship between this structuring and our interpretation of the work in the last chapter, so the general principles will not be unfamiliar. By offering a specific foreground-background organisation, the critic will help us to grow familiar more rapidly with the work; he may pick out features of the work that relate to a tradition of works with which we are already conversant; this may dissolve some of the initial strangeness. An art critic might show how, in Olympia, Manet both used and reacted against a tradition of the reclining nude from Titian to Ingres. Or a music critic might show how Britten speeds up the venerable device of the Alberti bass in the *Rape of Lucretia* so that, usually background, it becomes foreground. A work which, on the first encounter, seems an undifferentiated mass, thus becomes intelligible once we have signposts; the foregrounding by the critic provides us with the signposts.

As I have already hinted, that material selected as foreground will differ according to the place the critic occupies *vis à vis* the tradition. I turn again to some examples from music, particularly valuable here because they present a relatively enclosed development owing much less to outside influences from society than does literature, theatre or film. We can compare critical notes on Beethoven's *Fifth Symphony* by Tovey with those of E.T.A. Hoffmann, one of the very few early critics who offered an analysis in any way detailed. But although there are some differences in the passages picked out as of unusual power or originality (foregrounded), it is very difficult to tell whether the differences reflect different perspectives deriving from the different positions in the history of music on which these writers stand, or whether they merely reflect differing personal taste. And yet if there are differences in the way a work appeared to its first audience and the way it appears to us now, say two centuries later, it must surely be in the relative positions in the foreground-background hierarchy which given passages appear to occupy. And there is, I believe, inductive evidence for this in our own experience of how our impression of a work changes after we have heard other music.

As well as the Gestalt in which the work is seen, the listener contemporary with the work may differ from his successors in his estimate of the scale of the work and on this Tovey is illuminating,

Contemporary critics throughout Beethoven's career were continually deceived about the scale of his designs, or they would not so constantly have considered Beethoven inferior to Mozart in power of construction. With the rarest exceptions they always listened to a work of Beethoven in the expectation that its proportions would be those of a work of Mozart; and the mere measurement of the actual length of the work as a whole would not suffice to correct that assumption, for several very perfect works of Mozart may be found which are considerably longer than some characteristic great works of Beethoven. The enlargement of the time scale is not a matter of total length; it is a matter of contrasts in movement.[5]

He goes on to examine two of Weber's most celebrated criticisms of Beethoven, and in his analysis of the *First Symphony* he points out that Beethoven's contemporaries were surprised by the prominence of the wind writing and by the famous mixed tonality of the opening. Neither of these is so striking for a later generation, familiar as we are with the gamut of Beethoven's music. Our knowledge of the tradition of music modifies our view of an individual work. We can render intelligible to ourselves the scale of Beethoven's works because of our knowledge of a tradition of on the whole lengthening symphonies and larger scales. In this way we are enabled to organise the work and, ultimately, to judge it. And perhaps we may look no further for one reason as to why great music is not always appreciated by its contemporaries.

One testable consequence of this account is that we would expect to find certain works remaining in the repertoire until their bridging function has ceased. Thus we would expect that some music would be necessary in order to make intelligible the achievements of the succeeding generation but that once the style has become familiar, the music might not possess enough intrinsic interest to survive. The music of Stamitz and the other Mannheimers might have stayed in the repertoire long enough for the new classical style to be absorbed and then to have dropped out. Naturally enough this would be a fairly haphazard process and it might be difficult to distinguish it from the simple process of weeding out, through repeated hearings, the genuine from the meretricious. Parallels are not so easy to find in the other arts, largely I suspect because the factors that make verse, prose or film intelligible are manifold; literary arts after all use the language which we speak and the relation to earlier writers is but one of the conditions which make a particularly difficult poem at length intelligible. But it may well be that Eliot's *Waste Land*, which seemed for so long a 'difficult' poem, became intelligible to its first readers, those who were particularly interested in contemporary verse, through its relation to the poets who influenced Eliot — La Forge, Mallarmé, Verlaine and Pound. On the whole the problem of 'difficulty' is not the same in verse as it is in music and painting.

In one way the original audience was privileged. It could see immediately what was novel in a work in a way which we cannot. The response of the 'learned' did not depend upon acquiring a knowledge of the period and of the accepted style in order to recognise a striking innovation. What requires labour and scholarship on our part required no great effort on theirs. And when we learn the necessary background, our response cannot be as spontaneous.

In another way, of course, we are privileged for we can see what a work leads to. Admittedly the original audience might have guessed the lines of development which proceeded from Haydn and stimulated later generations. But although in this way the original audience's hearing may come closer to the modern, differences must remain; for one thing the great master may show us aspects of the tradition that we lesser musicians were never likely to see (and, possibly, close our eyes to others). Who, prior to Tippett and Britten, would have guessed the revivifying force of Purcell? And Alan Walker points out that Schoenberg's techniques have altered the way in which we examine the structure of past music! The French critic Riffaterre describes the ideal reader, who takes into account both the influences on a work and the influences that work has in turn on other, later works, as Super-reader. The musical paragon I have hinted at here could be called Super-listener.

I believe it would be a mistake to adopt such a creature as an ideal towards which we humbler beings should strive. The ideal of Super-critic is not compatible with what we know of the role of art in the individual life. Suppose I am invited to enlarge my taste, and am introduced to a writer with whom I had not previously been familiar, just as listeners of my generation have acquired a knowledge of Mahler and Elgar which would have seemed quite unlikely a decade and a half ago. It often happens, as a consequence, that our taste changes and we develop a liking for this particular style. Such changes of taste are tantamount to a conversion. A man's taste is an important part of the sort of person he is, and equally important, of the sort of person he sees himself as being; in the jargon of the psychologist his self-image is involved. The nature of a person is such that his taste in the arts is selective; it is part of my identity, in the looser sense of that term, that I love certain works and admire but do not love others; I admire *Don Giovanni* and *Emma*, but love *Pride and Prejudice* and the *Marriage of Figaro*. 'Tell me the books you read, and I will tell you what sort of person you are.' Hume observed, 'We choose our favourite author as we do our friend, from a conformity of humour and disposition. Mirth or passion, sentiment or reflection; whichever of these most predominates in our temper, it gives us a peculiar sympathy with the author who resembles us'. Equally we may avoid certain works in case, by coming to like them, we change in a way we regret. Not only do I not like Wagner, I do not want to like him. There is a famous anecdote of Rimsky-Korsakov advising Stravinsky against hearing the music of Debussy on the grounds that he might end up by liking it.

Even more strongly it can be argued that the concept of Super-critic is not a consistent conception. In the last chapter I argued that certain 'readings' of a work were mutually incompatible. The foregrounding of episodes which sustain one interpretation of *Hamlet* may be different from those which sustain another. Again one might imagine circumstances where, of two themes in counterpoint, either might be foregrounded. Although one could recognise the possibility of these two alternatives, either as possible interpretations in the hands of the performer or as possible 'concretions', clearly one cannot simultaneously hear them or perform them in the two different ways. Yet presumably it would not be enough for Super-critic to know of these alternatives: he would need to experience them for his experience to be at its richest. And this is not possible.

What turns upon the notion of a tradition? In its light I shall make the promised refinement of the simple consensus theory. As we have seen, the simple consensus theory enables me to distinguish the works I like from those which impress my peers. I may, of course, recognise technical expertise in a work which fails to move me, but without recourse to the consensus I shall be unable to distinguish those which are merely technically accomplished from those which also display the imagination and life which we look for in works of greater worth.

Secondly, it enables us to distinguish between works of quality and the rest without embarking on the dubious business of establishing criteria of artistic worth employing specific and identifiable properties present in the former but not in the latter. As I observed earlier, the history of such attempts has not been a happy one. Finally, it is worth recapitulating that this dependence on what Samuel Alexander called 'the conspiracy of the qualified' does not commit us to the view that the condition of a work having quality is that it impresses the connoisseur. It is quite compatible with the centrality of assent that the work possess properties which make it impressive even though no general principles can apparently be laid down exhaustively listing the precise combination of properties required. Realism is not compromised.

What qualifications do we require in a member of the peer group, those so qualified that their assent on question of taste matters? Hume suggests practice amongst others. But we also expect some degree of conformity with the rest of the consensus; if an individual's judgement diverges at every or at a majority of points from the consensus then he scarcely qualifies. We are equally hesitant about the critical judgement of one who suddenly conceives an extraordinary enthusiasm for the novels of Ford Madox Ford or for the poetry of Gerard Manly Hopkins if he simultaneously displays little or no knowledge of George Eliot, Dickens or Conrad, Keats or Browning. Hume pointed out that such an individual has not read enough to make comparative judgements and that that is disqualifying. But another and more important reason is that critics of limited experience may not know what is important in these works; their assessment of foreground and background or their judgement of scale may be faulty because they do not know how the work stands in relation to a tradition.

Thus, an intelligent response to Haydn's *Military Symphony* may involve our noticing an abrupt modulation where a bridge passage is usual, or monothematicism in a Haydn quartet where a second subject is to be expected. This connects with the way in which our knowledge of the development of the art may make us select certain features of the piece as central and thus organise our hearing of the work. In the ugly jargon of Ingarden a particular 'concretion' may be influenced by our knowledge of where the work stands in the tradition thus enabling us to foreground certain elements and place others in the background.

The upshot of these arguments is that the situation is a good deal more complicated than we would expect from the consensus theory unadorned. The complex theory which is now beginning to emerge assumes that the verdict of the consensus establishes a tradition which is itself a determining factor in the way we respond to a work, for from it we derive our conception of the expected, the usual and the standard in a style, and are thus able to understand and appreciate innovation. In addition, of course, once a creative artist has a place allotted by the consensus he is in a position to influence others and his status is doubly assured if only because his work is familiar. Indeed yet another reason for revising the accepted theory is that it seems likely that in music and theatre the performers have a greater say in what constitutes the consensus than either critics or the educated public.

The individual judgements and the consensus thus interact in a way which has become familiar in the course of our investigation of the interpretative process. Just as the detail of interpretation both controls and is controlled by the overall interpretation it supports and exemplifies, so the consensus is determined by the collection of individual judgements which qualified critics make; yet in turn it exercises a control on those judgements through the way the critical mind is formed. A critic develops his taste and judgements by reading, seeing or listening to works of art. What is available is determined by what a previous generation has thought worth making available. From time to time, of course, this picture of the achievements of the past is changed by the work of an authoritative voice. But the task of revaluation is always partial and always against the tide of his peers.

The verdict of the consensus reaches us in the convenient form of a tradition. We see the history of eighteenth-century music as a series of mountains, foothills and plains. Bach is flanked by Handel and, at a lesser height, by Scarlatti and Vivaldi. The mid-eighteenth century is much of a plain relieved by the smaller eminences of the sons of Bach and the Mannheimers until we reach the twin peaks of Haydn and Mozart; a caricature, no doubt, but it is the backcloth to our earliest experiences of music. In English poetry the heights of Pope and Dryden are not again equalled until the publication of Wordsworth's *Lyrical Ballads*. So, to summarise, although a viable account of critical judgement requires, as far as I can see, a reference to what has variously been described as the 'peer group', 'the consensus', or the 'assent of the qualified', the connection between the individual judgement and the verdict of the consensus is reciprocal. On the one hand the individual judge demonstrates his qualifications by the measure of his agreement with the consensus, on the other that understanding of the individual work which logically must precede sound judgement requires reference to that canon which has already satisfied the judgement of the connoisseurs, the canon now enshrined in the tradition. Yet the tradition itself is the product of the consensus. This, then, is what I called the complex assent or consensus theory and it requires, as we have seen, a conception of the tradition distinct from that of art history.

EPILOGUE

Earlier in this book I described the neo-Wittgensteinian thesis that 'art' is a 'family resemblance' concept as a proposal to be accepted only *faute de mieux*. The idea, you may recall, was that the various arts which are banded together under the generic title 'work of art' have no defining feature, no essence, which can be cited in an attempt to state necessary and sufficient conditions for the application of the concept. Rather, there are a number of overlapping features which some forms of art may have and others lack, which may be present in some cases and absent in others, and which go to make up disjunctively the content of the concept of art.

Have we found any alternative to this rather disappointing conclusion? The stress I place on interpretation in this book suggests that I think of art as the creation of objects which the public can interpret. This does seem to me a particularly important or central feature of art. However at least two objections need to be considered. First, the very same thing might be said of many other objects. Are not examination questions, crossword puzzle clues, statutes or deliberately hermetic books like those of Nostradamus or, arguably, the Gospels, objects for interpretation? Secondly, many uncomplex works of art are only interpretable in a very minimal sense, if at all. Not all works of art are like the stories of Henry James or the symphonies of Beethoven. The scope for interpretation in Schubert's *Heidenroslein* is relatively small. The interpretative questions in a border ballad are often too slight to make 'interpretability' a very plausible general element in our analysis. After all, if 'interpretation' is central to the concept of art then the job of interpretation cannot be trivial with respect to our response to the work. And yet, with many works of art, folk songs for instance, talk of interpretation seems absurdly tendentious.

Is there any way of resisting these objections? Let us note first of all, the idiosyncrasies of interpretation in the arts. First of all, the counterexamples in the first objection, examination questions, crossword puzzles etc., are cases in which a correct or right answer is possible. Statutes are not normally intended to be ambiguous, crossword puzzle questions only very exceptionally have more than one correct answer, and hermetic texts conceal a secret message. Art, by contrast, sustains multiple interpretations, no one of which is necessarily the only correct interpretation. This was, as we saw, a very significant and central feature of art. It may still be argued that examination questions may permit a variety of intelligent answers: their formulators may well be delighted at the ingenuity of a student who produces an unexpected answer. But we need to bear in mind as well the structure of interpretation. I argued that the variability of interpretations depends mainly on the variety of possible readings of a complex object, each different reading presenting a different view of the significant elements in the object. Readings characteristically differ as they present different foregroundings. An interpretation then explains the reading by offering a discursive account which takes cognizance especially of those elements which are important. Now ideally the foregrounded elements pick out what pleases or interests the reader whereas the student is not required to take an especial pleasure or interest in those implications of the examination question which his answer draws out. It is part and parcel of this approach to art that the connoisseur assumes that there are internal coherences which his interpretation registers and which emerge especially in the foregrounded elements. Other critical work may enable him to deepen and revise his view of the work and see this work in relation to its predecessors and successors in the way described in the last chapter. Consequently his maturing taste is revealed in the way his readings and interpretation approach the consensus. Thus in the complex response to art many of those aspects of aesthetic attention which we thought needed to be preserved can be seen to play a part. Given, then, the special form which interpretation takes when its object is a work of art there seems no reason to reject the general thesis that works of art are objects of interpretation.

Now the second group of counterexamples are examples where we seem to be dealing with more peripheral forms of art. Collingwood's distinctions can help us here. If we think that a Mozart divertimento is scarcely an object for interpretation it is because we think it is more properly classed as entertainment, and not as a work of art at all. The same goes for a Schubert waltz, or some of the more accessible songs. The centre of the concept of art is determined by the peculiarities of 'high art'. Entertainment and possibly political and some religious art may lie on the fringes. This does not mean that they are less valuable, of course. Many objects of aesthetic value which are not art count as more valuable than some indifferent works of art. The point about art is that it combines a sensuous appeal with intellectual demands and my account of interpretation is an attempt to do justice to that.

Works of art are not merely objects *of* interpretation. Many objects are objects of interpretation. Works of art are also created or presented as candidates for the peculiar form of interpretation described here. As good a conclusion as any is the slogan, 'Works of art are objects *for* interpretation'.

Notes

Chapter 1

1   Roger Taylor, *Art: An Enemy of the People* (Harvester, 1978).

2   Su Braden, *Artists and People* (Routledge & Kegan Paul, 1978).

3   A Marxist classic is Ernst Fischer, *The Necessity of Art* (Pelican, 1964). Lee Baxendall, *Radical Perspectives in the Arts* (Pelican, 1972) is also very irritating.

Chapter 2

1   P.O. Kristeller's famous paper, '*The Modern System of the Arts*', appeared in two parts in *The Journal for the History of Ideas*, vol. 12 (1951) and vol. 13 (1952). There are many testimonies to the power of music, from Plato in *The Republic* (349) to J.S. Mill, *Autobiography*, chapter 5.

2   For a brief historical introduction to aesthetics, the first part of George Dickie's *Aesthetics; an Introduction* (Pegasus, 1971) is both compact and lucid. The standard history of the subject is M.C. Beardsley, *Aesthetics from Classical Greece to the Present* (MacMillan, 1966).

3   M.C. Beardsley's views on the nature of aesthetics are to be found in his *Aesthetics: Problems in the Philosophy of Criticism* (Harcourt, Brace & World, 1958). My quotation comes from pp. 3-4. The entire book is a mine of information, and probably the most encyclopedic survey of aesthetics in recent years.

4   The quotation from Peirce comes from *Collected Works*, vol. 4, para. 537. For other discussions of the type-token distinction, see R. Wollheim, *Art and its objects* (Cambridge University Press, 1980); my 'Type, Token, Interpretation and Performance', *Mind* (July 1979), contains further references. I recommend Wollheim's book as the outstanding post-war contribution to aesthetics. Although I frequently disagree with it, it has influenced my thinking on many of these topics.

5   Spike Hughes, *The Toscanini Legacy* (Dover, 1970), p.380.

6   On forgeries, Goodman's discussion is in *The Language of Art*. (Oxford University Press, 1969).

7   Mark Roskill is very interesting on both the general question and the van Meegeren forgeries in particular in *What is Art History?* (Thames & Hudson, 1976). Students may find Colin Radford, 'Fakes', *Mind* (1977) interesting.

Chapter 3

1   The passage from Wittgenstein may be found in the *Philosophical Investigations 67.* Its application to aesthetics has been advocated by many writers. One of the most accessible is W.E. Kennick in 'Does traditional aesthetics rest upon a mistake?' in *Mind*, 1958, often reprinted. Other defenders include Paul Ziff and Morris Weitz whose *Hamlet and the Philosophy of Criticism* (Faber, 1965) will interest students whose main concern is literature. Weitz is, however, rather repetitive.

2   George Dickie's theory is developed in his *Aesthetics: an introduction* and with more subtlety in *Art and the Aesthetic* (Cornell, 1974). Note his discussion of the nature of an artefact. There have been many discussions of this theory in the journals. An example of a relatively recent work whose authors probably did not intend to write a book which would be viewed as a work of art is that masterpiece of comic fiction, *The Diary of a Nobody*. Wollheim too mentions how collections of material were shifted from the ethnology to the fine arts section of museums at the turn of the century when interest developed in Primitive Art. Dickie (*Aesthetics; an introduction*)

is persuasive on aesthetic attention and lucid on 'distancing'. Stevenson's distinction between dissective and synoptic attention is to be found in 'On the analysis of a work of art', (*Philosophical Review*, 1958). Wittgenstein makes some of the points about resemblance and representation which I use here, as does Nelson Goodman. Indispensable on these topics is E.H. Gombrich's *Art and Illusion* (Phaidon, 1960) which every educated person should have read. Perhaps the most useful general study of these topics is a collection of three essays *Art Perception and Reality* by Gombrich, Max Black and Hochberg. (Johns Hopkins U.P., 1970).

3   Jerome Stolnitz; 'On the significance of Lord Shaftesbury in modern aesthetics' appeared in the Philosophical Quarterly (1961).

4   The quotation from Murry comes from *Antony and Cleopatra: a selection of critical essays*, J.R. Brown (Ed.) (MacMillan, 1969).

5   Alan Walker, *A Study in Musical Analysis* (Barrie & Rockliff, 1962), contains the quotation from Schoenberg and much else of interest.

6   The subject of dramatic representation and illusion has been widely debated recently. Readers may find Howard Mounce, 'Art and Reality', *Philosophy* (1980) interesting.

7   According to Aaron Scharf, *Art and Photography* (Pelican, 1979), which is indispensable for this topic, a writer in the *Quarterly Review* (1846) seems to have been as early an advocate of what I call the photography model as anyone else; certainly it was common currency by the middle to the end of the century. (Gombrich's *Art and Illusion* is also *de rigueur*.)

8   Scruton's paper appears in *Critical Inquiry* (1981). The position he takes could, I think, have been forecast from the reading of his influential *Art and Imagination* (Methuen, 1974). I have also learnt from David Novitz, *Pictures and Their Use in Communication* (Nijhoff, 1977).

9   The most recent presentation of the linguistic analogy is found in Nelson Goodman, *Languages of Art* (Oxford University Press/Bobbs Merrill, 1968), but it is perhaps more familiar

from Wittgenstein *Tractatus, 210ff,* where picturing is offered as a model of language, rather than vice versa as here.

10   The quotations from Johnson are from *Preface to Shakespeare.*

11   I also quote from Sidney, *Defence of Poetry,* and Shelley, *Defence of Poetry.*

12   On fictional statements, the recent literature has been considerable. I have used David Lewis's 'Truth in Fiction', *American Philosophical Quarterly* (1978), apart from standard works on denotation, Russell's *On Denoting*, and Strawson's *On Referring*. The topic is also interestingly discussed in Nicholas Wolterstorff, *Works and Worlds of Art* (Oxford University Press, 1980). David Caute's very interesting *The Illusion* (André Deutsch, 1971), has been strangely ignored by literary theorists and philosophers. I have also used Patrick Cruttwell *The Shakespearean Moment* (Random House, 1960); Ernst Fischer, *The Necessity of Art* (Penguin, 1964); and David Daiches, *Critical Approaches to Literature* (Longman, 1971). R.J. Elliot's 'Poetry and Truth' appeared in *Analysis* (1967); and Beardsley's *Aesthetics* is also very helpful.

Chapter 4

1   An excellent brief account of what is sometimes known as the 'Idealist' theory of art is John Hospers', 'The Croce-Collingwood Theory of Art', *Philosophy*, (1956). Collingwood's *Principles of Art* has been reprinted by Oxford (1978) in paperback; Book I is essential reading. A useful anthology is J. Hospers *Artistic Expression* (Appleton Century Crofts, 1971).

2   The quotation from I.A. Richards comes from his *Principles of Literary Criticism* (Routledge & Kegan Paul, 1960).

3   Deryck Cooke's *The Language of Music* has been reprinted as a paperback by Oxford University Press (1962).

4   The quotations from Stravinsky are from his 'Poetics of Music' (1940) and *Expositions and Developments* (1962).

5 Hanslick's 'On the Beautiful in Music' (translated by Cohen) is published by Bobbs Merrill (Indianapolis, 1959).

6 Gurney's *On the Power of Sound* (Basic Books 1966; first published 1880) is extremely long and very repetitive but the aforementioned book by Hospers contains an excerpt. A causal theory of expression is defended by Khatchadourian in *The Concept of Art* (New York State University Press, 1971) and Guy Sircello's *Mind and Art* (Princeton, 1972) is also worth investigating.

7 On the basis on which we ascribe words like 'sad' to music see John Hospers' 'Art and Reality' in Sidney Hook (ed). *Art and Philosophy* (New York, 1964). See also Alan Tomey, *The Concept of Expression* (Princeton U.P., 1971).

Chapter 5

1 Lest any reader should think the textual and interpretive questions are easily distinguished, see L.C. Knights, 'Shakespeare and Shakespeareans', *Explorations* (Peregrine, 1964).

2 Joseph Margolis' 'Describing and Interpreting Works of Art' first appeared in *Philosophy and Phenomenological Research* (1961), and is reprinted in F.J. Coleman, *Contemporary Studies in Aesthetics* (McGraw Hill, 1968).

3 Wollheim's Leslie Stephen Lecture, 'The Sheep and the Ceremony', was published by Cambridge University Press (1979).

4 E.D. Hirsch, *Validity in Interpretation* (Yale University Press, 1967).

5 Wimsatt and Beardsley's paper first appeared in *Sewanee Review* (1946), and was reprinted in W.K. Wimsatt's *The Verbal Icon* (1954).

6 My discussion is largely based on Beardsley's discussion in *Aesthetics: Problems in the Philosophy of Criticism* (Harcourt, Brace & World, 1958). Amongst the many discussions of this

topic, I have found particularly useful Frank Cioffi, 'Intention and Interpretation', *Proceedings of the Aristotelian Society* (1963-4), repr. Cyril Barrett (ed.) *Collected Papers in Aesthetics* (Blackwell, 1965); Beardsley's later *The Possibility of Criticism* (Wayne State University Press, 1970) and Colin Lyas' 'Personal Qualities and the Intentional Fallacy', in G. Vesey (ed.) *Philosophy and the Arts*, Royal Institute of Philosophy Lectures, vol. 6 (1971-2), (MacMillan, 1973). See also Anthony Saville, 'The Place of Intention in the Concept of Art', *Proceedings of the Aristotelian Society* (1968-9).

7   D.A. Traversi, 'The Conflict of Passion and Control in *Henry V*', in Michael Quinn (ed.), *Shakespeare: Henry V: a casebook* (MacMillan, 1969), p. 155.

8   My information on *Hamlet* comes largely from M. Weitz, *Hamlet and the Philosophy of Criticism* (Faber, 1972); and J. Jump (ed.) *Hamlet* (MacMillan, 1969). Theories about interpretation are usefully distinguished in Richard Shusterman, 'Logic of Interpretation', *Philosophical Quarterly* (1978).

9   The example from Empson comes from the opening of *Seven Types of Ambiguity* (Chatto & Windus, 1970).

10   On *The Merchant of Venice* and *Henry V*, I have consulted MacMillan's casebook series, edited respectively by John Wilders (1969) and Michael Quinn (1969).

11   E.M.W. Tillyard. *The Epic Strain in the English Novel* (Chatto & Windus, 1967),pp. 132, 137, 159.

12   Leavis' essay 'The Europeans' is reprinted in D. Hudson (ed.) *English Critical Essays of the Twentieth Century*, 2nd series (1958). A very funny parody of Marxist interpretation is in Rosa and Charley Parkin, 'Peter Rabbit and the *Grundgrisse*', *Radical Philosophy* (1975).

13   On Prague Structuralism, see P.L. Garvin (ed.), *A Prague School Reader* (George town University Press, 1964) and Frederick K. Jameson, *The Prison House of Language* (Princeton University Press, 1974) gives some of the background to these developments.

14   Max Black's 'Metaphor' first appeared in *Proceedings of the Aristotelian Society* (1954-5), and is reprinted in Coleman, op. cit. W.B. Stanford, Greek Metaphor (Blackwell, 1936) is another classic. Two further papers from which I have learnt are: R.J. Damaan, 'Metaphors and Other Things', *Proceedings of the Aristotelian Society* (1977-8); and Donald Davidson, 'What Metaphors Mean', *Critical Inquiry* (1978). Black's most recent contribution appears in 'More about Metaphor', in A. Ortony (ed.), *Metaphor* (Cambridge University Press, 1978).

15   The quotation from Steiner comes from *On Difficulty* (Oxford University Press, 1978), p.22.

16   For the curious, the performance of Prince Gremin's aria from *Eugene Onegin* comes from the recording conducted by Rostropovitch.

Chapter 6
1   The issues involved in aesthetic uniqueness are clearly discussed in Levinson's eponymous article 'Aesthetic Uniqueness', *Journal of Aesthetics and Art Criticism* (1980).

2   The two quotations are from Margaret MacDonald and Arnold Isenberg, in William Elton, (ed.), *Aesthetics and Language* (Blackwell, 1959).

3   A. Hutchings, *Schubert* (Dent, 1945), p.101.

4   L.B. Meyer, *Explaining Music* (University of California Press, 1973), p. 219.

5   Donald Tovey, *Essays in Musical Analysis,* vol. II (Oxford University Press, 1973), p.5.

Other material I have found useful includes:

Sibley's influential paper 'Aesthetic Concepts', *Philosophical Review* (1959), which has been much reprinted. O.G. Sonneck (ed.), *Beethoven: Impressions by his Contemporaries* (Dover 1967); Wayne Booth, *Rhetoric of Fiction* (University of Chicago

Press, 1966); V.F. Perkins, *Film as Film* (Penguin, 1972); and Tony Bennet, *Formalism and Marxism* (Methuen, 1979), Students should also read Hume, On the *Standard of Taste*, vol. 1, (ed. Greene and Grose, 1882, complete edn).

INDEX

Abraham, Gerald 173
Aesthetic, compared with art 8–9
Aesthetic attention 36–49
Aesthetic attitude 36–49
Aesthetics, definitions of 10–12
Aesthetics, origins of the
    concept 8
Alexander, Samuel 179
Aristotle 6, 86, 154
    Poetics 6
Armstrong, Louis 121
Art, the historical development of
    the concept 6–7
Art, what its forms have in
    common 27–60
Art-world theories 30–6
Arts, the classification of 6–26
Attention, dissective and synop-
    tive 45–6
Austin, J.L. ii
Autographic and allographic 20
Automatization 172
Avison, Charles 93

Bach, J.S. 119, 126
Balzac, Honore 3
Bartok, Bela 119
Baumgarten, A.G. 8
Baxendall, Lee 187
Beardsley, M.C. 11, 26, 121,
    123–32, 150, 155, 168, 187,
    190, 192
Beauty and aesthetics 10
Beethoven, L. van 164, 173
    Symphony no. 1 175
    Symphony no. 5 126, 174
    Symphony no. 6 93

Symphony no. 7 173
Symphony no. 9 44–5, 126–7
Waldstein Sonata 139, 147
Bennett, Tony 194
Berlioz, Hector 106
    Harold in Italy 173
    Irlande 106
Black, Max
    On representation 63, 189
    On metaphor 149–59, 192, 193
Booth, Wayne 87, 193
Boulez, Pierre 127
Braden, Su 2, 187
Bradley, A.C. 42, 132, 138
Brahms, Johannes 106
    Sextet in G major 144
Brecht, Berthold 51–2
Britten, Benjamin 177
    Rape of Lucretia 174
Brook, Jocelyn
    Orchid Trilogy 155
Brooks, Cleanth 123
Browning, Robert
    Andrea del Sarto 161–2
Bullough, Edward 47–9
Burke, Edmund 10

Cage, John 32
    Silent Music 30, 171
Cardew, Cornelius 35
Cardus, Neville 168
Carner, Mosco 173
Carter, Elliot 41
Cause and object of emotion 114
Caute, David 87, 190
Cavell, Stanley 171
Cioffi, Frank 191–2

Class and art 1–5
Coleridge, S.T. 42, 156
Collingwood, R.G. 94–8, 185, 190
Communication and art 149
Conformism and art 149
Connolly, Cyril 75
Conrad, Joseph 86
    Nostromo 85, 140–2
    The Secret Agent 122–3
Consensus, in evaluation
    Chapter 6 *passim*
Constable, John 72, 74
Conventional and natural signs in
    music 100–2
Cooke, Deryk 99–112
Criticism, reasons in 141–9
Croce, B. 94–9, 190
Cruttwell, Patrick 87, 190
cummings, e.e. 155

Daiches, David 190
Damaan, R. 151, 193
Davidson, Donald 151, 193
Debussy
    Jeux 17
Density 42–6
Dickens, Charles
    Hard Times 136–7
    Nicholas Nickleby 79
Dickie, George 8, 30–6, 187, 188
Dilthey, W. 146–7
Disinterestedness 37–9, 91
Distancing 47–9
Donne, John 87, 155
Dummett, Michael 83

Education, aesthetic 145–6
Elgar, E.
    Symphony no. 2 127
Eliot, George 9
    Middlemarch 9, 13
Eliot, T.S. 21, 153, 170–1, 176
Elliot, R.J. 91, 190
Empson, William 135, 153, 156
Expressionism Chapter 4
    passim, 148

Family resemblances 28–30

Fergusson, Francis 132
Fictional counterfactuals 79–81
Fictional statements 75–92
Film 26, 71–2
Fischer, Ernst 87, 187, 190
Flaubert, Gustave
    Madame Bovary 164
Foregrounding 142–7, 172–8, 184
Forgery 20–4
Freud, Sigmund 46
Fry, Roger 98–9
Furtwangler, Wilhelm 131

Gainsborough, Thomas 164
Gardner, Helen 132
Garvin, P.L. 192
Giotto 65
Goethe, J.W.v. 86
Gombrich, E.H. 72–5, 189
Good likeness 64–75
Goodman, Nelson 20, 24, 63, 180,
    189
Guinness, Alec 53
Gurney, Edmund 104, 191

Hall, Peter 17, 117
Hanmer, Thomas 132
Hanslick, E. 101–7, 169, 191
Hardy, Thomas 3, 86, 122
Harris, Frank 124
Haydn, Joseph 163, 164, 179
Hepburn, Ronald 107
Hermeneutics 141–9
Hirsch, E.D. 120, 128–30, 191
History of Art, as contrasted with
    tradition 168–81
Hochberg, Julian 189
Hoffman, E.T.A. 174–5
Honneger, Arthur
    Pacific 231, 93
Horace 89
Hospers, John 97, 190
Housman, A.E. 124
Hume, David 56, 178, 179, 194
Hutchings, Arthur 167
Huxley, Aldous 155

Idealist theory of art 94–8

Illusion in the theatre 50–6
Ingarden, Roman 22, 173, 180
Intentions 121–32
Interpretation of art 86, 116–60
  as condition for 'high art' 183–5
  and textual meaning 130
  two forms of 116–17
  variety of 132–41
Isenberg, Arnold 91, 165, 193

James, Henry
  Ambassadors 87
  Europeans 142–3
  Princess Casamassima 128
  The Turn of the Screw 122
Jameson, Frederick 192
Janacek, Leos 109
Johnson, Samuel 50, 75, 89, 132, 134, 190
Jones, Ernest 132, 138
Joyce, James 130

Kant, Immanuel i
Kaplan, David 58–61
Karajan, Herbert v. 17, 127
Keats, John 89
Keller, Hans 117
Kennick, W.E. 188
Kerman, Joseph 26
Kermode, Frank 130, 147
Khatchadourian, Haig 191
Klemperer, Otto 120
Knights, L.C. 191
Kott, Jan 120, 132
Kristeller, P.O. 6–7, 187

Lawrence, D.H.
  The Rainbow 89–90, 121
Leavis, F.R. 142–3, 192
Levin, Harry
  The Intelligent Heart 90
Levinson J. 193
Lewis, David 79–85, 190
Literature, its ontology 15–16
Lyas, Colin 192

MacDonald, Margaret 165, 193
Mahler, Gustav 106, 131

Manet, E.
  Olympia 136, 174
Manner in music 109–15
Mannheim School 176
Marceau, Marcel 53
Margolis, Joseph 119, 191
Marvell, Andrew
  The Horatian Ode 87, 125
Marxism and art 1–5, 87–8
Maturation of aesthetic taste 39–42
Maxwell Davies, Peter
  St Thomas Wake 114
Mendelsohn, Felix
  Italian Symphony 105, 173
Messiaen, Olivier 131
Metaphor 149–59
  As statements 158
  Interaction theory 150–4
  Uses of 149, 158
Meyer, L.B. 174, 193
Mill, J.S. 187
Milton, John 82, 97, 116
  Comus 147
'Mixed arts' 25–6
Moore, Marianne 92
Mounce, Howard 189
Mozart, W.A. 94, 104, 105, 119
  Marriage of Figaro 3
Mukarovsky, Jan 172–4
Murdoch, Iris 84
Murry, John Middleton 42–3, 189
Music and emotion 93–115
  and interpretation 16–20
  and language 99–112
  natural and conventional signs in 101–2
  and representation 93
  its recognition as an art 7
  work and performance 16–20

Nietzsche, Friedrich 130–1
Novitz, David 189

Opera 26
Originality of art 163
Orwell, George
  Animal Farm 91

Painting, ontological status of 11–13

Passmore, J.A. 10

Peirce, C.S., on type and token 14, 15, 188

Performance and interpretation 115–19

Perkins, V.F. 194

Perspective 67

Photography and representation 66–74

Picasso, Pablo 140

Pictorial representation 56–75

Plato 6, 8, 187
Ion 6

Plotinus 8

Poetry and performance 19

Possible worlds 76–84

Pound, Ezra 155, 156

Practical criticism, its dubious intellectual pretensions 21–22, 171

Pretending 50–5

Prokofiev, Serge
'Lieutenant Kije' 83

Puccini, G.
Turandot 85

Purcell, H. 177

Pushkin, A. 123

Radford, C. J. 188

'Reading, concept of 143–9

Representation 49–92
and causality 58–61
and convention 66–75
of emotion 93–115
and intention 61–4
and language 66–7
in literature 75–92
and resemblance 56–8

Reynolds, Joshua 164

Richards, I.A. 98, 150, 190

Riffaterre, M. 177

Rimski-Korsakov, N.A. 178

Ripa, Cesare
Iconologia 61–2

Roskill, Mark 23, 188

Rules of judgement in art 163–8

Russell, Bertrand, theory of descriptions 77–88, 190

Ryle, Gilbert 9, 154

Scharf, Aaron 74, 189

Schoenberg, Arnold
First Chamber symphony 46, 177, 189

Schubert, Franz
C major symphony 126, 127, 173
Octet 174

Schweitzer, Albert 94–5

Scruton, Roger, on photography 69–70, 189

Selection in criticism 146

Serly, Tibor 119

Shakespeare, William 180, 183, 190, 193
Antony and Cleopatra 42
Hamlet 117, 118, 120, 132–4, 138–9, 142
Henry V 124
Macbeth 153–4
The Merchant of Venice 138–9
A Midsummer Night's Dream 17, 117
Othello 47–8, 50, 54
Sonnet LXIII 135, 153

Shelley, Percy Bysshe 76, 190

Shusterman, Richard 192

Sibley, Frank 193

Sidney, Sir Philip 75, 190

Similes 149–59 *passim*

Sircello, Guy 113

Solomon (the great pianist, not the sage and womaniser) 131

Song 25–6

Sonneck, O.G. 193

Spark, Muriel
The Prime of Miss Jean Brodie 59

Stanford, W.B. 152, 193

Steiner, George 154, 193

Stevenson, C.L. 45, 189

Stieglitz, Alfred 69

Stolnitz, J. 37, 189

Stravinski, Igor 100, 111, 117,

127, 190
Strawson, P.F. 78–9, 190
Structuralism, Prague variety
  143, 170–8
Superreader and supercritic 177
Sussmayr, Franz 118–19
Swift, Dean
  Gulliver's Travels 91

Taylor, Roger 1–5, 187
Tchaikovski, P.I. 106
  Eugene Onegin 155, 193
Tillyard, E.M.W. 140–1, 147, 192
Tolstoi, Leo 98–9
Tormey, Alan 191
Toscanini, Arturo 17–18, 120
Tovey, Donald 170, 175
Tradition and history in art
  169–81
Traversi, Derek 124, 192
Truffaut, F.
  Fahrenheit 451 16, 40
Tunes of glory 53
Type and token 13–26, 145

Uniqueness in art 164, 166
Unity in art 43–5, 164
Universals 14

van Meegeren 21–4
Vasari 75
Villa Lobos, Hector
  Little train of the Caipira 93

Wagner, Richard, his conception
  of music drama 26
Wain, John 22
Walker, Alan 189
Weber, Carl Maria von, 175
Webern, Anton 128
Weitz, Morris 133, 188, 192
Wilde, Oscar 163
Williams, Bernard 50–1
Wilson Knight, G. 120, 132–3
Wimsatt, W.K. 121, 191
Wittgenstein, L. 9, 28–30, 109,
  188, 190
Wollheim, R. 120, 188, 191
Wolterstorff, N. 190
Woodhouse, A.S.P. 147, 192

Zelenka, J.D. 41–2
Zeuxis 65–6
Ziff, Paul 188
Zola, Emil
  La Bête Humaine 84